To Tara,

Hope you enjoy
the memoir

Very best
Freddie

URBAN NOMAD

A Memoir

URBAN NOMAD

A Memoir

FREDDIE KELVIN

Tread Softly Press

First Edition

Published by Tread Softly Press,
a venture of freddiesfotosforever.com.

Manufactured in the United States of America
ISBN: 979-8-8427-5634-6

Cover and interior design by Sheila Hart Design, Inc.
www.hartsart.net

Cover photo part of the collected works by Freddie Kelvin.
More images can be viewed at freddiesfotosforever.com.

For my family

Family Tree

Names of relations that appear in this book

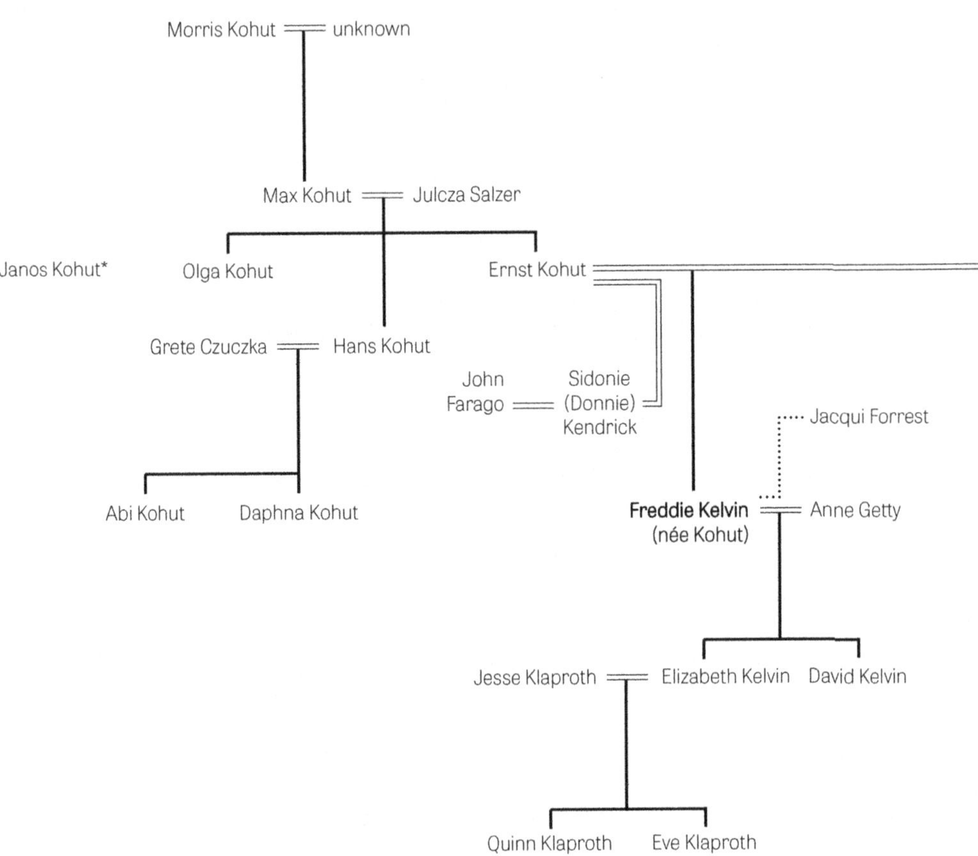

* cousin to Ernst Kohut, link unknown

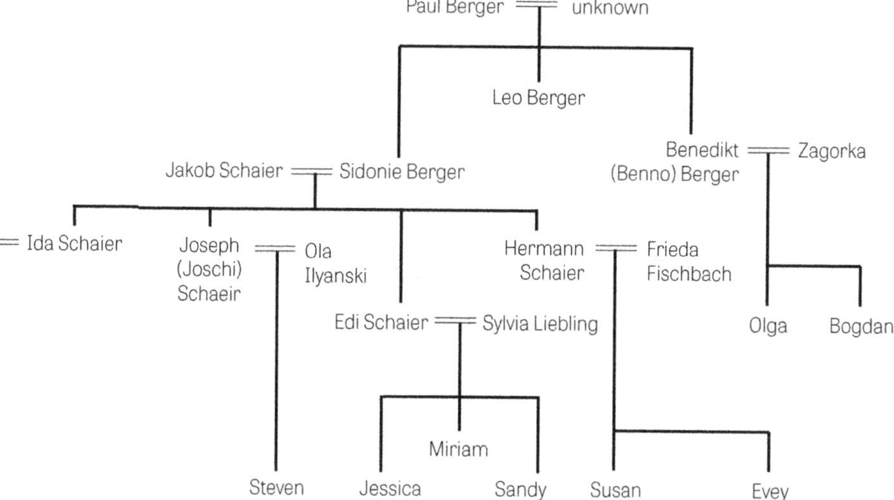
Paul Berger
unknown
Leo Berger
Jakob Schaier
Sidonie Berger
Benedikt (Benno) Berger
Zagorka
Ida Schaier
Joseph (Joschi) Schaeir
Ola Ilyanski
Hermann Schaier
Frieda Fischbach
Edi Schaier
Sylvia Liebling
Olga
Bogdan
Miriam
Steven
Jessica
Sandy
Susan
Evey

Table of Contents

Part One

MY FAMILY'S HISTORY AND LIFE IN AUSTRIA

My Father's Family and Background

My father Ernst Kohut was born in Vienna, Austria, on January 16, 1905, the oldest child of Max Kohut and Julcza Salzer. Max Kohut was born in Letnicie, a small village of about 500 people, near Bratislava, in Slovakia. Max's father, Morris "Mor" Kohut, owned some kind of a pub there with a garden that contained a few fruit trees. Not surprisingly, my grandfather Max wanted to seek a better life and somehow made his way to Vienna, which must have seemed a world apart from where he grew up. His wife, my grandmother Julcza, was one of seven siblings. One of her sisters, Karolin, was even more prolific than her, for she gave birth to 10 children. As a result, the family tree exploded. Beyond that, despite resorting to Ancestry.com, I know little more about my father's forebears. If only my father had told me more about his grandparents, my family history would have been so much more meaningful.

Vienna was one of the world's first truly multi-ethnic cities. The heart of a strained and over-extended Austro-Hungarian Empire, it glittered with prosperity even as hundreds of years of Habsburg family inbreeding took its toll on the ruling family. While the family itself started to crumble over the course of the eighteenth and nineteenth centuries, at the turn of the twentieth century the empire still encompassed a long list of European countries. This diversity gave rise to a capital city that was as deeply innovative, artistic and intellectual as the Habsburgs were staid and traditional.

Approximately 175,000 strong, Vienna's Jews played a highly important part in this creativity. Most of the city's lawyers and physicians were Jewish, as were many of its journalists and businessmen. The key to their prominence was partly attributable to the high proportion of Jewish students at the Gymnasia, Vienna's elite secondary schools. Jews accounted for 30 percent of Gymnasium students, despite only constituting 10 percent of the population. Their contributions to music, literature, visual arts, and medicine were immense. Among the most prominent Jewish figures of these times were Sigmund Freud, Gustav Mahler, Arnold Schoenberg, Stefan Zweig and Theodor Herzl, the founder of modern Zionism.

But, as ever, this relative peace and prominence would not last for Vienna's Jewish community. In the year of my father's birth, Karl Lueger was mayor of Vienna. He is considered to be the father of modern political antisemitism. His populist campaigns against the city's Jewish minority were so notorious that, when he was first elected mayor, the emperor refused to endorse him. It was he who gave rise to the infamous "Lueger March" in which people all over the streets of Vienna gathered to sing: "Lueger will live and the Jews will croak." In due course, Lueger became a major influence on an unsuccessful artist who was living in Vienna at the time. You may have heard of him. His name was Adolf Hitler.

When my father was in his eighties, we persuaded him to record his impressions of life in Vienna, so we are fortunate to have a detailed account of the many years that he spent in the city of his birth. For most of the time that I knew him, he was loathe to display his feelings too openly. In these taped recordings, however, he released an abundance of warmth and sensitivity in a manner that was quite at odds with the father that I had come to know and love.

My grandfather Max built a shoe factory in Vienna. It is not clear how that fledgling business grew into a very successful operation, for my father did not recount any of those details. However, it appears that my grandfather's factory was among the first in central Europe to make shoes using machines, thereby replacing work that had previously been done by hand. As a result of their success in the shoe business, my paternal grandparents eventually came to live on the fourth floor of a new apartment block which, according to my father, was the finest in the Seidengasse (Silk Street). Of course, he could be forgiven for being ever so slightly biased in this assessment.

The apartment overlooked the city's rooftops and provided a view up to the distant high hills of the Vienna Woods, which formed the northeastern corner of the Alps. My father, his older sister Olga, and their younger brother Hans were taken care of very well. They had a governess who took them to the nearby parks and (hopefully) taught them good manners, and Olga and my father received piano lessons from a well-known teacher, even performing at piano recitals.

In the taped recordings, my father gleefully recalls the day that he rebelled against the daily grind of these lessons and painted the teacher's piano stool with ink. This brought an immediate halt to any further piano instruction, which I think must have pleased him no end.

For many of their childhood years, my father and Olga spent enjoyable summer vacations in Perchtoldsdorf, a charming small town 10 miles from the city center on the edge of the Vienna Woods. The town had two swimming pools, tennis courts and, at one end, a castle belonging to an archduke which was, of course, strictly off limits. My grandparents diligently visited their children in Perchtoldsdorf every evening and returned to Vienna early the next morning in order to manage the shoe factory. In those days, with slow transport, this must have been quite a time-consuming ordeal.

When World War I started, my grandfather was called up and initially declared fit for combat. Fortunately, because of chronic stomach issues, he never saw action. Instead, he was transferred to a desk position in the Censor Department of the military where he could put his knowledge of multiple languages to good use. Consequently, he was again proud to look distinguished in his civilian clothes, which were expensively designed by first-class tailors.

Oh my, that shoe business must really have flourished! From the few photographs that I have of my grandparents and the family, the importance of being fashionably dressed is abundantly clear. World War I ended, of course, in 1918. As a result, the vast Austro-Hungarian Empire dissolved and this brought to a halt the long-lasting, inbred and very out-of-touch rule of the Habsburg dynasty. My father was 12 at the time. He makes no comment about how this momentous defeat affected his life in Vienna. Perhaps, like many teenagers, he was too caught up in the details of his own existence to pay attention to what was happening all around him.

My father had passed the entrance examination for the prestigious Realgymnasium when he was 10 or 11 years old. Several aristocrats were students there, including Prince Lobkovitz whose family home was the baroque Lobkovitz Palace. One of this prince's ancestors had been a devoted patron of music and was himself a musician. Beethoven was a regular guest at his palace and conducted the first public performance of the Eroica Symphony there. At the Realgymnasium, my father enjoyed learning French, German, history, and geography, but did not care for chemistry or mathematics. I think those learning (or non-learning) genes were passed on to me. My father was a good, but not outstanding, student at the Realgymnasium. He did not make many friends there, perhaps because he was not academically inclined. I suspect he could handle the aristocrats, but I'm not sure that they could handle him as he could be quite cynical.

On leaving the Realgymnasium, he enrolled in the Academy of Economics where he learned administration, finance, organization, and took other courses that had practical applications. While carrying out these studies at the age of 15 or 16, he also worked in the family shoe factory. There, he learned how every department functioned, first as an apprentice, and then as a foreman. He became, in time, a very capable shoe designer. His broad-ranging experience in the family factory would pay off in spades later in life.

My grandmother went to the factory every day where she handled all the administrative duties. The family therefore had to have a cook, and she prepared all their meals. My grandfather was rather strict and would not tolerate any bad behavior at the dinner table. Accordingly, my father was sometimes sent to his room with barely anything in his stomach. Later in the evening, however, my grandmother would bring food to his room while, at the same time, admonishing him to show better manners.

In 1917, my father's older sister Olga, who was then 14 years old, developed acute abdominal pain but was too embarrassed to undress and allow the handsome young doctor at the summer camp to examine her. As a result, her diagnosis was unfortunately delayed. When she finally underwent surgery, doctors found that she had developed peritonitis due to a perforated appendix. She died four days later.

Until this point in time, my father's family had been devoutly religious Jews, but this tragedy shattered them and resulted in their abandonment of any semblance of religious practice. If God could allow such punishment, they decided, then worshipping God was no longer for them. Though this led to my father no longer practicing his faith, he nevertheless always retained strong links to his many Jewish friends in the community. In those days, remaining culturally Jewish while abandoning Jewish ritual was far less common than it is now. Jews were not highly assimilated, so their religious practice was a very strong binding force. My father's irreligiosity had a striking impact on me and would later come to have a major influence on how I viewed myself as a Jew.

Despite this renouncement of religious practice, my father did have his bar mitzvah the following year. The synagogue was full. About 50 relatives came, as well as many business and "coffee-house" friends. It appears that the guests had been given a list of books from which to choose as bar mitzvah presents, because my father received many books of German and Austrian classics but none of these were duplicated. The only book by a foreign author was a translated work of Oscar Wilde's, who was to become one of my father's favorite authors.

With the dissolution of the Austro-Hungarian Empire at the end of World War I, the map of central Europe was strikingly redrawn. Poland, Hungary and Romania became independent countries, Bohemia and Slovakia merged to become Czechoslovakia, and the federal state of Yugoslavia was created, to be ruled later by Marshal Josip Broz Tito. My grandfather's shoe company had agents in all these countries but, with the break-up of the empire, the shoe products now had to be exported abroad rather than sold within the confines of the Habsburg Empire. In 1918, my father's younger brother Hans was born.

He was strikingly handsome, so much so that my grandparents feared that he might be kidnapped by gypsies. From photographs I have seen, I would venture to say that my father was just as handsome!

My father had become an excellent swimmer and was soon to join the sports club "Austria," where initially he was made to feel very welcome and made many good friends. He became a member of their water polo team and was told that, if he trained hard, he might be able to make the Austrian Olympic team. He was, however, no longer interested in devoting inordinate amounts of time to training.

On one occasion, the club's water polo team travelled to Bratislava to play the Czechoslovak national team. The club won both matches and their players became concerned that they might be attacked during the night by members of the losing team. The Czechs, having freed themselves from the Habsburg yoke, retained a strong hatred of Austrians and were looking, instead, to establish relationships with Britain and France. My father frequently participated in local swimming competitions, as well as some that were international, and won a considerable number of medals, some of which I now have in my possession. Incidentally, at one of these events, a relatively unknown guy named Johnny Weissmuller broke the world record for 100 meters. Despite his years of fun and success at the sports club "Austria," my father left the club in 1933 because it was becoming openly antisemitic. He would go on to join the well-known Jewish sports club, Hakoah, which had been formed in 1909 partly because Jews, in those days, were excluded from joining other sports clubs.

One time, my father participated in a swimming competition at the opulent Hotel Excelsior on the Venice Lido and won both the 100 meter freestyle and 200 meter breaststroke, as well as being a member of the victorious water polo team. After these gratifying events, he was photographed in the company of some of the hotel's upscale summer guests and had occasion to meet a young lady named Daisy. They subsequently saw each other on quite a few occasions. However, being wary of continuing to date a non-Jewish girl against the wishes of his mother, he felt compelled to terminate this otherwise happy relationship.

Sporting activities were a large part of my father's social scene. Outside of work, he joined a tennis club, where he became good friends with many of the players. Together, they would spend many happy times in nearby restaurants as well as frequenting a variety of coffee houses (from what I can tell, this seems to be what all Viennese did...all the time). He also attended lectures by Alfred Adler, a psychoanalyst who, after parting ways with Sigmund Freud, famously went on to introduce the concept of the inferiority complex.

At one of Alfred Adler's lectures, my father met a young woman named Lilli who, following the lecture, was going on to attend a rehearsal of Mahler's Eighth

Symphony, the so-called "Symphony of a Thousand." However, choir members never come close to that exaggerated number whenever this symphony is performed. More because of Lilli than Gustav Mahler, of whom he was unaware, he joined her at the rehearsal. This experience was of great significance, for it marked the beginning of my father's unending love affair with classical music.

Lilli was also a member of a claque at the Vienna State Opera. A claque member was paid by opera singers to clap and shout approval at appropriate moments following their arias, in order to whip up the remainder of the audience to do likewise. Not paying for a claque could be devastating to an opera singer, as the ordinary public then didn't feel under any obligation to applaud. From that time onwards, for two or three years, my father accompanied Lilli to the state opera approximately three times a week. They both sat in the back of the auditorium, where she conscientiously followed the score. Although my father could not read the score, he was nevertheless, over the course of time, able to sing many of the arias by heart. Despite Lilli and my father spending so much time together at the opera, he declared that the two of them never met even once anywhere outside the opera house. I somehow doubt that this was the case!

Later on, through a friend in the famed school of Max Reinhardt, the wonder boy of European theater after World War 1, my father obtained free tickets for well-placed seats at the state opera under the guise of being a music critic. What chutzpah! (For those unacquainted with this Yiddish term, it roughly translates into "sheer nerve and cool effrontery." These seats, obviously, were far preferable to sitting in the back of the auditorium. He attended many other concerts of classical music in a variety of locations, where he enjoyed symphonies, piano and violin soloists and, often, lieder. He was particularly fond of lieder. These are German poems set to music and sung by a soloist with piano accompaniment. With lieder, the poem is often itself a great work of art, known and loved without the music.

My father also enjoyed the theater and continued to spend time in the company of his friends from both the swimming and tennis teams. His frequent fascination with opera, classical music and the theater inevitably reduced his involvement in water polo matches. Austria regarded soccer as far more important than other sports, so my father attended some of the country's major games. On one occasion, he went to Budapest to see Austria play Hungary. Walking around that city, he came across a beautiful girl stepping out of a Rolls Royce. Her name was Zsa Zsa Gabor. It appears that she addressed everyone as "Dahlink" (and why not?). Despite being a mediocre actress, she famously (or infamously) married nine times, often to aristocrats or extremely wealthy men. She once aptly declared: "I am a marvelous housekeeper. Every time I leave a man, I keep his house."

In 1930, my grandmother Julcza Saltzer died after a long battle with breast cancer. She had been a wonderful mother to my father as well as a selfless wife to my grandfather. During World War I, it seems that she played a pivotal role in keeping the shoe factory running while my grandfather served as a military censor. It was a very sad time for the family, for she was clearly loved by all.

At some early point in his youth, my father discovered skiing. Once he had bought the necessary equipment, he and his friends went skiing nearly every weekend from December to May. He was particularly friendly with Schakerl Dvorak, who had been the backbone of the water polo team of the club "Austria." My father tried his hand (and body) in bobsleigh competitions during which he was lucky to escape without any serious injury. When in a major city like Innsbruck, my father and Schakerl would contact the local clubs with water polo teams. They were delighted to have the two well-known players help their members in training sessions.

Another close friend was Laci Fischer, a charming guy who was the major salesman for the factory and displayed a very strong affinity for the many women he encountered during and after his business journeys. Laci's father was well known, for he was one of the main cantors in Vienna. My father also became involved in other sports, including sailing and a crude form of water skiing, both of which took place on Lake Worthersee. Despite working long hours in the factory, he had an ever-increasing list of activities from which to choose in the evenings, as a result of which he was rarely at home later in the day.

Reflections on My Father's Early Life

It is abundantly evident that life in Vienna for my father was a whirlwind of wonderful experiences. I find it interesting that he placed a great deal of emphasis on the sports that he played. There is no question in my mind that he was proud of his achievements in these activities. In view of this, I wonder why he did not pursue the opportunity to play water polo for his country. It seems he was deflected from this goal by other interests that he had developed. In particular, he had come to love classical music and opera, and I think these new avenues on land were clearly a source of conflict with those that took place in the water. He was able to take full advantage of the cultural scene in Vienna, and I suspect that he has passed a smidgen of these traits on to me.

While dwelling on sporting activities and the cultural scene, he shared very little of his feelings about relationships, except for tragic events affecting his family. He barely described any details of his role in my grandfather's factory, even though it was to become substantial. I see my father as someone who tended to hide his feelings, except when a family member passed away. Perhaps this was typical of the era. Whatever his true feelings were, I sense that he cared deeply about his immediate world. He was someone that I will always revere.

My Mother's Family and Background

My mother, Ida Schaier, was born in 1911 in Klagenfurt, the capital city of the southern Austrian province of Carinthia. Klagenfurt boasts a Mediterranean climate, is beautifully situated on the eastern bank of Lake Worthersee, and is surrounded by dramatic mountainous landscape. Despite Mahler retreating there to compose much of his music, it was something of a cultural wilderness. There were no lectures by prominent psychoanalysts and no state opera performances to enjoy. In contrast to Vienna, with a population of some two million persons and more than 175,000 Jews, Klagenfurt's population at the time was around 100,000, of which only approximately 200 were Jewish. By 1968, only 10 Jews were still living there. I think you get the picture!

My mother was the second youngest child of Jakob Schaier and Sidonie Schapira, both of whom came from Galicia, an impoverished region in the far northeast of Austria which was annexed by that country in 1772. Jakob was born there in 1882. His parents left Galicia, like so many others, because of dire economic conditions. One year after his birth, widespread pogroms took place, and these gave rise to further waves of emigration. Between 1881 and 1914, approximately 350,000 Jews left Galicia. My grandfather and his parents found their way to Klagenfurt, where he grew up. Given the very limited availability of Jewish bridal candidates there, he was sent on a marriage mission back to Galicia where he was given the choice of three brides for a shidduch(a Jewish arranged marriage). His choice, as mentioned above, was Sidonie. In addition to my mother, Jakob and Sidonie had three more children: first Joseph or "Joschi," then Hermann, and finally Edi.

Unlike my father, who recorded his life in detail when he was in his eighties, I have no similar information from my mother, who died at the untimely early age of 46. To make this lack of remembrance even worse, I was in denial of my mother's death and therefore have very few recollections of her. However, my amazing 97-year-old aunt Sylvia, the surviving wife of Edi Schaier, was both able and very willing to provide a good deal of information about the Schaier family during the last year of her life. The subject of the conversations with her daughter Miriam and me was, very naturally, related mainly to Edi's life. Nevertheless, Sylvia gave us considerable insights into the Schaier family's existence in Klagenfurt. Fortunately, I have access to Sylvia's conversations with us on a flash drive given to me by Miriam. I also received valuable information about the Schaier family from Evey, Hermann's younger daughter.

Jakob Schaier had attended business school and owned a clothing store near the railway station in Klagenfurt. The family lived in a house above the store and in its early days, farmers brought fruit and vegetables which were kept in the store's cellar. Every market day, farmers could trade their produce for shirts or other clothing...which sounded like a good deal.

Easter was always a difficult time for the Schaiers, because the local priests would get their congregants riled up against the Jews, in the hope of making their lives more uncomfortable. Nevertheless, with the passage of time, the business was very successful and became the largest department store in Klagenfurt. Because of the demands needed to run the store, the family required several helpers in their home, as well as a maid. It is not clear to me what they all did, but I imagine that they performed a wide variety of household tasks. Later, the family moved their store and home to the Alterplatz, the main pedestrian street in Klagenfurt, which was lined with historic buildings as well as restaurants, cafes and shops. I suspect that this new location was much better for business.

According to Sylvia's reflections on Edi's life in Klagenfurt, all of my mother's and her siblings' friends were Jewish. There could not have been that many Jewish children in their age group, though! Edi was a good sportsman and was on both the school ski and handball teams. When he was a senior, he took a school trip down the Danube and the Rhine rivers. During these travels, the schoolboys stayed in the homes of German families. When the hosts opened their doors, Edi was greeted with many salutes of "Heil Hitler," as Hitler's rise to power had already begun.

On Edi's return to Klagenfurt, his "school-issued" skis were confiscated because he was Jewish. To remain on the school ski team, you had to use these school-issued skis rather than your own. He was then informed that he could no longer be on the school ski team because he didn't have the school set! Such brilliant thinking on the part of these antisemites. Never underestimate their cunning! According to Sylvia, Jews were never accepted in Klagenfurt because antisemitism had always been very much part of the fabric of the community. Many of the townsmen carried Nazi symbols on the inside of their jacket lapels.

Such cowards! One time, during a medicine ball game, Edi was actively harassed for being Jewish. His response was to bring the heavy ball down on the kid's head. Apparently, that shut him up.

When Edi was 16 and my mother 19, Jakob bought a second store which became a shoe shop. The keys to this shop were handed to Edi and my mother and, together, they ran the store. Edi was still at the Gymnasium and my mother at business school so in the mornings one of them, presumably my mother, ran the store while Edi took over in the afternoons. Between them, they clearly carried a lot of responsibility for their age. Eventually, Edi was sent to Vienna to learn how to make shoes, a skill that was required at that time in order to sell shoes.

My mother's family were observant Jews. My grandmother Sidonie kept a kosher house but did not cook. Apparently, she oversaw the cooking and ensured that the food was cooked in the appropriate way. My mother played no role whatsoever in the kitchen and later needed to be taught these skills. According to Edi, my mother was quite an independent person. She was always stylishly dressed, for her clothes invariably came from Vienna.

It is not clear what my mother and her siblings did for recreational activities, but both she and Edi were better skiers than my father, so obviously that was one sport in which they participated. Edi also enjoyed ice skating on the canal that connected Lake Worthersee to the town of Klagenfurt.

In 1936, when Sidonie Schaier was 46, she decided to have surgery to reduce the excess fat in her lower abdomen. She and Jakob selected a well-known Viennese surgeon to carry out the procedure. Tragically, she developed a blood clot postoperatively which eventually led to her death. My father already knew her very well and was very much affected by her passing.

Sidonie had two brothers, my great uncles. One was Leo, who was a playwright that tried his luck in Vienna without success. The other was Benedikt "Benno" Berger, who was later to play a critical role in my parents' lives. My uncle Hermann met Frieda Fischbach while both were students in the Gymnasium, and they subsequently married. Hermann was, fortunately, in the last law school class to accept Jews, and had even obtained a job in Vienna. Frieda had earned a Masters of Business Administration, or the Austrian equivalent thereof. During their time in Austria, neither Edi nor Joseph married. Perhaps, as in Jakob's case, this was because there were only a limited number of Jewesses in this neck of the woods from whom to choose.

Clearly, Vienna and Klagenfurt, although in the same country, were worlds apart. Although I can hazard a guess at some of my mother's experiences, I often wonder how much my mother's formative years must have differed from my father's. Despite many instances of antisemitism, Vienna was a beehive of artistic and intellectual activity which was, to a considerable extent, pollinated by a highly educated community of Jews. There was no opportunity in provincial Klagenfurt for this to occur and, even if it did, it would almost certainly have been suppressed. With Jews constituting only one in 500 persons of the population there, it is no wonder that they were considered aliens. The fact that my mother's family was very observant Jews could only have added flames to the already burning fire.

When my cousins visited Klagenfurt after the war, they saw the site of its synagogue which had been destroyed during Kristallnacht. It had become a parking lot. A memorial to the synagogue had been constructed but was largely hidden by the parked cars. The memorial had both German and Hebrew inscriptions. The German inscription reads as follows: "In memory of the life of suffering of our former Jewish fellow citizens. Here stood their house of prayer. It was destroyed under the National Socialists in 1938." Isn't "the life of suffering of our former Jewish fellow citizens" a rather hypocritically pious piece of phraseology?

The Hebrew transcription strikes a rather different and far more sordid note: "The place you are standing on is holy ground…a synagogue that was intentionally destroyed by the wicked Nazis in the terrifying and awesome night of Kristallnacht in the year 1938." Fortunately for the Austrians, most of them probably cannot read Hebrew. Klagenfurt, at least on the surface, has since overcome its notorious past, and now welcomes tourists from central Europe and far further afield, including Israel! They come to enjoy its climate, scenery, and the warm alpine Lake Worthersee. It is also host to a wide variety of cultural events. It can keep them all for, as far as I'm concerned, I will never set foot there.

Ernst Meets Ida

Vienna was noted worldwide for its elaborate and festive balls. More than 400 of them took place every winter. These balls ranged from the most aristocratic of events such as the Vienna Opera Ball to the more accessible Confectioners' Ball (for those with a sweet tooth), and even a Laundrymaids' Ball. My father only attended three of these events as many were highly exclusive and expensive affairs.

The last of these three balls was organized by the Jewish sports club, Hakoah. Historically, the club had several thousand Jewish members for it was the social hub for many Viennese Jews, and a place that stood firmly for Jewish solidarity, pride and self-confidence. At this ball, my father's good friend Laci Fischer introduced him to a young lady named Ida Schaier. She was the daughter of one of my grandfather's shoe customers in Klagenfurt. My father went on to spend the entire evening in her company.

After the ball, they stayed very much in contact with each other. My mother would come to the factory in Vienna to place orders for her family's shoe store, and she and my father would go to the theater and enjoy many happy times together. Several months later, in June of 1936, they were married and embarked on a honeymoon in Venice.

On the train to Venice, they met a young man who was a Baron von "something or other." While he was pleasant company, he clung to them like a leech. He was extremely useful, however, when they wished to eat at a smart restaurant, for the maître d' would always find a table for them even if the place was fully booked.

Following their return to Vienna, they moved into a beautifully furnished apartment which my wife Anne and I saw when we visited Vienna in 2009. Both from the outside, which sported many attractive balconies, and from the entrance, with its delicate metalwork, it was clearly an elegant place for my parents to start their married life.

Soon after their marriage, my mother's uncle Benedikt "Benno" Berger brought his daughter Olga to Vienna. Seeking more opportunity for his burgeoning career in dentistry, Benno had previously moved from Klagenfurt to Belgrade, the capital of Serbia. There, he rose to become a professor of dentistry at the University of Belgrade and met and married a charming Catholic lady named Zagorka. In the process he, too, became a Catholic and so he brought five-year-old Olga with him for her to attend a Catholic school there. My parents, accordingly, took Olga out every weekend. They found her to be a delightful girl, and very much enjoyed their time with her.

I often wonder why my father says so little about my mother in the taped recordings. There is, for example, more about Zsa Zsa Gabor than her. I find this to be rather amazing and even a little upsetting. It seems that he enjoyed his encounters, brief or otherwise, with the so-called upper classes. Maybe that's the case with many Jewish people as they try to ascend the social ladder. I regard his and his family's break with religion when his elder sister Olga died so tragically to be of immense significance. Despite that, he felt obligated to marry a Jewish lady, for his mother insisted on this. Is it in any way ironic that an irreligious, cosmopolitan man would fall for a relatively devout woman "from the sticks?" Well, maybe this is yet another case of "opposites attract."

My paternal grandparents, with my father and his sister, Olga

My maternal grandparents, with my mother, Edi, Hermann, and Joschi

Club "Austria" water polo team with my father, far left

My parents' wedding, Vienna 1936

The Anschluss, and its Aftermath

All (relatively) good things are destined to come to an end. This was certainly true for my parents in Vienna and for my mother's family in Klagenfurt, although the social scene in Klagenfurt was never exactly an effervescent one for Jews. The fateful events that befell our families could well happen again if we fail to learn from the terrible times that they faced. Never doubt that discrimination remains alive, for it has always been a recurring part of the Jewish experience.

In July 1934, just a year and a half after Hitler had come to power in Germany, a group of Nazis seized the Austrian chancellery in a putsch, or coup, and attempted to overthrow the government. Although they failed in this, they nevertheless managed to assassinate the Austrian chancellor, Engelbert Dollfuss.

At this point, my father's younger brother Hans, a strong Zionist, wanted to leave Austria for Palestine. Unfortunately, my grandfather insisted that he stay, and the majority of the family supported this viewpoint. It was not until much later, in June 1938, that Hans left Austria and managed to find a place on a ship going to Palestine.

One month after the putsch, in August 1934, Hitler declared himself Fuhrer of the German Reich and thereby became the absolute dictator of Germany. In September 1935, the notorious Nuremberg Race Laws were passed. These laws robbed the Jewish population of essentially all civil rights. Unbelievably, at this time, the Nazis rejected American racist laws because they found them too harsh. Were they just whitewashing themselves?

In March 1938, German tanks and armored vehicles crossed the border into Austria and were enthusiastically received without any resistance whatsoever. In Vienna alone, 250,000 Austrians turned out to welcome Adolf Hitler who was, of course, their son come home. The following day, large swastika flags were displayed throughout the city, and raucous pro-German demonstrations took place everywhere. Austria's parliament was quick to formally approve the Anschluss (the country's annexation into the German state) and so Austria became a German province named Ostmark.

Not surprisingly, all antisemitic decrees were immediately applied to the new province. Unquestionably, the brutal persecution of Jews that followed the Anschluss was perpetrated mainly by Austrian Nazis, and not by their German "invaders." Austria loves to distance itself from Nazi violence by arguing that it, too, was a victim of Hitler's rise to power, but nothing could be further from the truth.

Persecution of the Jewish population started immediately after the Anschluss. Jews, including soldiers of World War I who even wore their uniforms complete with all the medals they had earned, were made to clean and wash the pavements and streets. The heads of Jews were shaved, and some had a swastika stamped on them. Jews were made to lie down and eat the grass, orthodox Jews were pulled around by their beards, and Jewish children were forced to write the word "Jud" on the windows of their fathers' shops. Far, far worse, many Jews were arrested in the streets, coffee houses, or their homes, and taken to prisons or concentration camps. In my mother's family, Joschi Schaier and his father Jakob were arrested at the railway station in Klagenfurt and kept in jail there for three months. What required several years to carry out in Germany happened overnight in Vienna!

Very soon after the Anschluss, a Nazi Schutzstaffel, or SS man, and three accomplices came to my grandfather's shoe factory and sent my mother home with an admonition not to return. My grandfather was told to leave his office. A chauffeur for one of the SS men occupied his chair, and then toured the factory with one of the foremen. The next day, a lorry with several SS men arrived and the entire stock of shoes, thousands of pairs, was removed. Shortly after, my father received a phone call from the family apartment to inform him that my grandfather, like hundreds of other Jews, had committed suicide. The recognition that his life's work had suddenly been torn away from him was too much to bear.

My father had no time to grieve, for he now found himself having to deal with many complicated and difficult issues. Many of the older factory workers expressed their condolences but were soon thrown out and replaced by young Nazis. All of this was happening so fast that my father could barely keep up with events. He was now expected to run the factory, partly because its Nazi occupiers were completely clueless and partly because the new financial controller hoped to later sell the factory for a much higher price. My father ensured that he travelled to and from the factory by car, for being on the streets meant that he could be transported away at a moment's notice.

It was not soon afterwards that my father picked up the phone and was told to report the following morning to the Gestapo's headquarters. He took just a toothbrush with him, obviously fearing the worst. Perhaps the toothbrush was symbolic of a healthy freedom but, nevertheless, it seemed an odd choice. As he entered the building, he saw Black Marias, or police vehicles, filled with Jews coming into the adjacent carpark and leaving without them. He was instructed to go to a particular room on the second floor. After knocking on the door and entering, he was confronted by two Gestapo officers. As he was sitting down, he saw a form on the desk saying: "Here appears the Jew Kohut." He was questioned as to whether he had a Swiss bank account and replied that he knew nothing about this. After several more questions, he was, to his astonishment, allowed to leave. However, before reaching the door, the Gestapo officer called out "Halt." My father thought this would surely be the end for him. The officer handed him a small strip of paper and then, with a wave of the hand, dismissed him. Shaking from head to foot, my father walked slowly down the stairs, not knowing whether he was heading for a Black Maria. This is the kind of stuff of which movies are made. He handed in the piece of paper and was told that he could indeed leave! My father could not understand why the Gestapo had let him go. After all, Jews were being arrested left, right, and center. From this moment on, he decided that he and my mother, as well as Hans, must leave the country, and as fast as possible.

Escaping Nazi Europe: My Parents and Uncle Hans

Accordingly, my father sent letters to four shoe companies offering his services and stating his skills. Two of these were in Australia, one in Canada and the remaining one, strange as it may seem, in Ecuador. He received replies from the two shoe companies in Australia. One expressed their delight, asked my father to bring skilled workers with him, informed him that he would need a medical certificate, and, in a short sentence at the bottom of the reply, asked about his religion. He saw a physician at the British Embassy to obtain the appropriate medical certificate. The physician there was Jewish and warned my father that the question about religion was a clear indication that the company would not accept Jews. The second Australian company sent a cable addressed, very fortunately, only to a "Mr. Kohut" stating that they would engage him. My father gave the cable to Hans, since he could fairly claim, in place of my father, to also be a "Mr. Kohut."

Hans, an ardent Zionist, took the cable to the British Embassy to get a visa. He planned to tell the consul there that he was going to start a job in Australia but would first go to Palestine to visit some friends before proceeding to Australia. There were, not surprisingly, hundreds of people waiting in line. My father and Hans showed the cable to a janitor, who immediately took them to the front of the long line. Hans walked into the consul's office alone with the cable and, shortly afterwards, emerged with a visa for Palestine. He and my father could not believe their luck! Hans was warned by two "Aryan" friends not to leave Vienna by train, as this would lead to his arrest, so he immediately took a flight to Trieste and from there sailed to Palestine.

My father had a cousin, Janos Kohut, who was headmaster of a school in

Banja Luka, the second-largest city in Bosnia. He had visited my parents in Vienna before the Nazi occupation and had agreed to look after my grandmother's jewelry which was hidden in the upholstery of one of their chairs. My mother's elder brother Joschi warned my father that Bosnia would not accept Jewish immigrants. To counter this threat, Joschi had concocted certificates for both himself and my parents which stated that they had all been baptized Catholic five years ago, the minimum required time for them to be acceptable. Since my father had only known my mother for two years, these certificates in the names of Mr. and Mrs. Kohut had no validity, but, fortunately, no one bothered to check them during their subsequent travels.

The next step for my parents was to get passports. The clerk to the family attorney went to the appropriate place to obtain them. She covered herself with swastikas which, no doubt, helped greatly in this matter. Very soon, my parents each became holders of precious German passports. The final document that was needed, of course, was an exit visa which stated that my parents had paid all their taxes and much more. My parents' faithful maid Wilma handled this in a rather clever way. She took her three kittens in a small bag to the office issuing visas and proceeded to put them on the desk counter. Even Nazi officials, I guess, will play with kittens if they are not contaminated with Jewish blood! The kittens caused quite a distraction and so she was able to obtain the visa without too much difficulty.

Meanwhile, my father's good friend Laci Fischer had arrived in Leeds, England, where his father had obtained a position as a cantor. Laci wrote my father that there was a shoe factory in Leeds owned by the Appleson brothers and that the brothers would find someone with my father's skills to be very useful. Laci strongly suggested that my father should come to Leeds before heading out to Australia. One arrow in my father's quiver was that he was a very talented shoe designer, in addition to his other skills.

My father made a list of which clothes he would take with him and, helped by his brother-in-law Edi, bought material to take to his tailor to make into additional items of clothing. He also visited his accountant, whose office was opposite the Gestapo headquarters. The accountant, still somewhat protected by being a Hungarian rather than an Austrian Jew, generously offered to take three crates of household items with him to the USA. My parents packed a silver tray, tea set, and bowls into the crates, as well as two small carpets and some bedding, but never expected to see them again.

Shortly after, in September 1938, the police came to my parents' apartment looking for my father. Fortunately, he was not home when they called. Hearing of their unannounced visit, my father resolved to leave immediately and took an Air France flight to Belgrade in Serbia, where my mother was scheduled to join him within the next several days. Two of my mother's three brothers, Hermann and Edi, as well as their father Jakob, elected to remain in Klagenfurt in the hope that they could save many of their possessions. Clearly, they were rolling the dice and taking an enormous risk.

As my father flew over Vienna, he felt a deep sense of relief, despite my grandfather's suicide and losing virtually all his possessions, believing that everything would now be alright. He felt confident, perhaps strangely so, since his wife was still in Vienna. "It is only after the deepest darkness that the greatest joy can come," said Malcolm X, and perhaps he was right. My father reflected on the love and care of his parents, especially that of his late dear mother, but also that of his father despite his sometimes harsh and strict manner. He realized that the discipline and sense of duty acquired from his father enabled him to handle and overcome many of the difficulties that he was now facing. He also remembered many of the good times in Vienna that were filled with sports, music, theater, warm friendships, and much more.

On arrival at the Belgrade airport, two policemen approached my father with the intention of arresting him and putting him in prison. They had received a phone call from the police in Vienna that he was an escaped Jewish refugee. This was unexpected, for he had not thought that Serbia was antisemitic and, moreover, the country had not yet been overrun by the Nazis. Fortunately, my mother's uncle Benno was there to meet him. Benno was not only a professor of dentistry but also a medical officer to the Danube Steam Ship Company, so the Serbian police listened to what he had to say. He gave them his assurance that my father would leave within 24 hours to go to Temerin, a small town in Serbia where his cousin Janos Kohut and his family lived. Nevertheless, when my father went to pick up his luggage, he was told that it would need to be examined and that this would not be a quick search. Benno said that the guys handling this were expecting some baksheesh, or bribe, so my father gave them half of the money he had managed to take with him and they then let him go.

My father enjoyed the freedom of an evening with Benno and his charming wife Zagorka in Belgrade, and the next day took the train to Temerin in Serbia where he was met by his cousin. There is some confusion here, because my father's earlier recording stated that Janos lived in Banja Luka in Bosnia, which is seven hours from Temerin. Perhaps the family had moved in the meantime, but this is unclear.

He was made to feel very welcome at Janos's home and, within a few days, my mother joined him. She said that the police had come by to pick up my father a day or two after he had left Vienna. By another stroke of luck, my father had now survived two most unwelcome visits by the Nazi police to their apartment.

They stayed with Janos's family for three months and were very well looked after. Towards the end of this time, both my father and Hans urged Janos and his family to leave Temerin and go to Palestine. Hans, of course, was already there.

Janos did not take this advice and stayed with his family in Temerin. Although the German army did not invade Yugoslavia until 1941, an ultra-nationalist organization composed of Croats, the Ustase, led by Ante Pavelic, progressively attained power. A fundamental goal of this Nazi puppet state was to eradicate Serbs, Jews, and the Romanis (gypsies). To this end, many concentration camps were established, the most notorious of which was Jasenovac. Overall, it is estimated that up to 600,000 Serbs, Jews, and Romani were murdered there. Their methods of extermination horrified even the Gestapo. Children were blinded, their eyes gouged out, or they were hacked to death with shovels. Men were hung upside down and castrated before being strangled or mauled to death by dogs.

Ante Pavelic and his senior officers survived the surrender of his party in 1945 and, citing their Roman Catholic faith, appealed to the Vatican for help. Shockingly, the Catholic Church obliged. Using clerical passports, the escaped Ustase officers made it all the way to Argentina along the infamous German "Rat Line." Pope Pius XII was hand in glove with the Ustase. It was he, after all, who had signed that fateful concordat which helped Hitler achieve unchallenged power in Germany. Most Westerners are blissfully unaware of all these events, for they have received little mention in the press. This enraged my father, who felt that Western civilization and its unalloyed allegiance to the Catholic Church, and Christianity in general, had given the Ustase an unequivocal and entirely undeserved pass. In the Balkan wars of the 1990s, the Serbs inflicted a terrible revenge on the Croats. What goes around comes around.

At some point after my parents left Temerin, Janos and all his family perished. There is no way of knowing whether they were eliminated by the Ustase or the Nazis. Perhaps they did not know of the bloodcurdling behavior of the Ustase in neighboring Croatia. But, surely, with the arrival of my parents from Austria, they must have been fully aware of the murderous atrocities being carried out by the German Nazis. If only they had heeded the advice of my father and Hans!

One might reasonably wonder why my parents lingered for three months in Temerin, given what they already knew and what they anticipated might next happen. My parents clearly needed to plan their next moves, which they hoped might, at last, bring them to safety. Because of the possibility of a job with Appleson's in Leeds, they decided to go first to London where, relying on a tourist visa, they could then buy a return ticket to and from Sydney, Australia. This, of course, required a large sum of money, far more than they had been allowed to take out of Austria. However, by selling some of my grandmother's pieces of jewelry that Janos had brought back from Vienna, my father was able to obtain sufficient cash to buy these tickets. He then took the train to Belgrade, despite the risk based on his experience at its airport, and went to the Thomas Cook travel agency to obtain the necessary tickets. Upon his return, Uncle Benno told him that Australia had issued a new rule that all tourists traveling to that country were required to have a permit from their consul before a visa could be granted. The Australian consul was very kind and gave visas to my parents that were stamped with a date prior to this new ruling.

To reach London, my parents first needed to pass through Italy, Switzerland, and France. When my father went to the French consul in Belgrade, he was, to his surprise, refused a French visa. As a result, my parents now had to take a train through Italy to reach Zurich in Switzerland. From there, they would fly to London, bypassing France in the process. It seems that a visa was not needed to travel through Italy, but Switzerland was an altogether different matter. In the fall of 1938, the German authorities required that all passports of German Jews (which now included Austrians, of course) had to be surrendered, and would become valid only after a large "J" had been stamped on them. On October 5, 1938, the Swiss and German governments had signed an agreement that all Jews, as indicated by the "J" on their passports, would no longer be able to enter Switzerland. This meant, of course, that my parents' path to freedom via Switzerland was closed, and that they would be doomed to return to Germany when they reached the Swiss border.

Nevertheless, my father, accompanied by Joschi, went to the Swiss embassy in Belgrade to try to obtain a visa that would allow them to enter Switzerland. The consul there, Mr. Glaser, was very helpful, and immediately granted them a visa that could be used only for a train journey at a specific date and time. The visa, however, required the signature of the Swiss ambassador, who, upon seeing the large "J," refused to comply.

My parents returned to Mr. Glaser with this disastrous information. He reached into his drawer and pulled out a strip of paper with the ambassador's signature on it. He said to my father: "Go ahead and sign the passport visa yourself." My father replied that he could not possibly do this, but Mr. Glaser assured him that this had been done on many previous occasions and that my father should go ahead. My father took the strip of paper and informed Uncle Benno of what had transpired. He told Uncle Benno that he, with shivering hands, could never sign the visa himself. Uncle Benno took a glass plate, put the strip of paper with the ambassador's signature under the plate, then opened the passport to the page with the visa, and proceeded, with a very steady hand, to sign the visa with a signature that mimicked that of the ambassador. What a relief! My father went immediately to the Thomas Cook travel agency to book the train to Zurich via Italy in accordance with the visa's timetable, as well as to obtain airplane tickets from Zurich to London.

When their train reached Milan, Italy, my parents found out that they needed to change to another train, contrary to what the agent at Thomas Cook's had told them. They managed to change trains, but not before seeing a Jewish family taken off the train to face a very uncertain fate. In Zurich, my parents boarded the flight to Croydon, near London. There, the immigration officer stamped their passports after seeing the visa for Australia which indicated that they would be leaving England within three days' time. The other Jewish refugees arriving in England by that plane were not so lucky. The British authorities sent them all back to Switzerland, from where they would presumably be deported to Germany. Laci Fischer and one of the Appleson brothers, Yank, were waiting at the Croydon airport for my parents and they went on to stay, greatly relieved, overnight in a London hotel before being driven to Leeds.

At a much later date, my father saw an atlas of Jewish history written by Martin Gilbert, later Sir Martin Gilbert, one page of which showed the number of Righteous Gentiles in each country. He had listed none for Switzerland. Upon seeing this, my father gathered documentation about Mr. Glaser, the Swiss consul in Belgrade, and sent the information to Martin Gilbert, who wrote him a very appreciative and detailed reply.

ESCAPING NAZI EUROPE: MY MOTHER'S FAMILY

The situation in Klagenfurt for my mother's immediate family was, perhaps, less complicated. There were, after all, only a small number of Jews living there. Despite this, the dangers were almost certainly of the same magnitude. I am indebted once again to my uncle Edi's extraordinary wife Sylvia for being more than willing to share the experiences of Edi and my mother's other siblings. Sylvia was, in a wonderful way, a strong mother figure to whom I always looked up and loved, even though we did not see each other that often.

Sylvia's narrative starts the day before Kristallnacht, which took place on the night of November 9, 1938. My parents had already fled from Austria and were, at that time, in Temerin, Serbia, staying with my father's cousin Janos. Joschi had moved on to the south of France, and Hermann and his wife Frieda were in Vienna.

If ever there was a turning point in the fate of the Jews in Austria and

Germany, it was Kristallnacht, the "Night of Broken Glass." On that night, and over the next 48 hours, hundreds of synagogues were destroyed, approximately 7,500 Jewish-owned businesses, homes, and schools were plundered, 91 Jews were murdered, and an additional 30,000 Jewish men were arrested and sent to concentration camps. While the major perpetrators were undoubtedly Nazis, large numbers of ordinary Austrians were involved in the looting and plundering. People of all ages turned out to humiliate Jews, and whole classes of schoolchildren were brought by their teachers to see the smoldering synagogues and jeering crowds.

There were many Austrians and Germans who were ashamed, and some even appalled, by what took place. In any nation or society, there are always a mixture of good eggs and bad eggs, although the proportions of each likely varies from country to country and is frequently influenced by the times in which they live. Too often, though, it is the bad ones who end up calling the shots, both literally and metaphorically.

Around the time of Kristallnacht, Edi and his father Jakob decided to leave Klagenfurt and take the overnight train to Vienna. They could not call Hermann to say they were coming because the phone lines were tapped. At the exact same time, Hermann and Frieda had left their apartment in Vienna and gone to Klagenfurt. Nevertheless, Edi and Jakob managed to gain entrance to Hermann's apartment. That day, there was a knock on their door and, opening it, they were confronted by two policemen. Fortunately, Edi, fearing the worst, had already pushed Jakob into a back room so that he was out of sight. The police said they had come for Hermann Schaier, because he was "on their list." Edi told them that he was not in the apartment. Hearing this, the police asked Edi for his name and demanded to see his passport. By now, of course, all Jews had a big "J" stamped on their passports. Seeing this, one of the policemen said, "Well, they want us to take one Jew, so you will do," and told him to come with them. On the way out, seeing Edi's coat hanging on the door, one of the policemen mentioned, "You'd better take that with you, because where you are going will be cold." Edi replied that he did not need it because he would soon be coming back to the apartment.

These police were Austrian police, not Nazis, and were likely just following orders. They took Edi from one police station to the next, picking up many Jews on the way, and finally arrived at a large prison. There, all the cell doors were open, and no one had been locked up. Edi felt an urgent need to get back to Jakob, who had already been in jail once. He went into one of the cells, took out his pen and a piece of paper, and proceeded to write a letter to himself, signing it with the name Uncle Benno. The letter he wrote, purportedly from Uncle

Benno, stated that he (Uncle Benno) had reserved a place for him at a medical school in Africa (naming a specific country, of course) and that he knew Edi was coming and was looking forward to his arrival. Edi took the letter to the guy in charge of the prison, who said, "Just get out of my sight, or I'll shoot you, too."

In the evening, a different Nazi took over running the prison, and Edi realized that he was a relatively nice guy, to the extent that this was possible. So, Edi got in line to see him and, looking very smart in his suit, showed him the letter that he had written. Fortunately, Edi's name was not on the list. The "nice Nazi" let him go on the condition that he was accompanied by Austrian police. As soon as he was out of the prison, he gave the police some money, whereupon they left him alone. He ran as fast as possible to Hermann's apartment, only to find that his father Jakob had taken an overdose of sleeping pills. He was unable to revive him, so he asked the concierge to find him a fiacre (a four-wheeled horse-drawn carriage). The driver of the fiacre was sympathetic and took them to a nearby clinic. Jakob recovered after a few days, and they took the train back to Klagenfurt.

The timing of these events is unclear. His daughter Miriam told me that when Edi was back in Klagenfurt, people who had been good friends asked him, "How did you come back from the dead?" and refused to acknowledge him. What is clear is that Austria had grown increasingly far more dangerous and hostile for Jews. While Edi had been granted an extension to stay in Austria, he and his father did not wait to leave, and set about completing their packing. They called a customs official so that he could check what was being packed. Before the official arrived, Edi had contacted the hotel next door and asked them to send over goodies that included, at least, goulash and beer. While the official busied himself with eating and drinking this handsome spread, Edi quietly kept packing as many items as possible into the trunk. Edi had previously taken some of his mother's gold jewelry, and had the gold melted down to make a cigarette case. Edi opened the case and offered the official a cigarette, all the while keeping the case in his hand because its weight would have given the game away. He took a cigarette himself, and then nonchalantly tossed the heavy gold case into the trunk which the official, having no idea about its nature and value, proceeded to seal.

Edi was extremely smart and, furthermore, was prepared to take risks. He owned a classic Puch 200 motorcycle, which was his most prized possession. He used to drive it from Klagenfurt over the nearby mountains into Italy, which gave him a great sense of freedom. One day, the Nazis came to take his motorcycle away. Surreptitiously, he removed its battery before handing it over. The next day, the Nazis returned with his motorcycle and demanded he restore the battery "or else." He did but, at the same time, put sugar in the gas tank hoping that this might lead to the bike exploding while being ridden. Few Jews would have had the nerve to pull off these stunts, especially in such times!

Jakob, and then Edi accompanied by his packed trunks, travelled by separate trains to Antwerp, Belgium. Jews were only allowed to take 30 Deutschmarks out of the country. En route, they reached the last stop in Germany, beyond which they would ostensibly be free. A Nazi official boarded the train and wanted to check that Edi had only the maximum allowance of 30 Deutschmarks on him. Unfortunately, they noticed that Edi had, in addition, some coins in one of his pockets, so they pulled him off the train and put him in jail. The trunks, though, stayed on the train.

The next morning, Edi was hauled before a judge who sternly told him that he wanted German, not "dirty foreign," money and he should get this meager amount exchanged for Deutschmarks. The judge allowed Edi to go to the bank around the corner from the courthouse to make the exchange. However, being concerned that this might lead to further complications, when Edi reached the bank he hung around until it was lunchtime, flipped the "open" sign to show "closed" and returned to tell this to the judge, who then let him go. When he got on the next train and finally reached Antwerp, he found, to his surprise, that all his trunks were at the railway station there.

He managed to meet up with Jakob, and together they looked for a hotel, many of which said: "Dogs and Jews not allowed." Helped by my mother, arrangements were made for Jakob to go to Leeds. Sylvia was unsure how Jakob was then able to reach the United States, but he did so by ship, arriving in New York City in 1940 or 1941. Edi stayed on in Antwerp for approximately a year. He survived there by giving English lessons to refugees who, understandably, no longer wanted to speak the German language. Eventually, he was able to board a ship that took him to England and relative safety.

At or just after Kristallnacht, the head Nazi officer responsible for administration in Klagenfurt rounded up all but one of the Jewish men there, including Hermann, and had them dispatched to the concentration camp at Dachau. It was bitterly cold there, and the inmates had only the equivalent of two T-shirts to cover their upper bodies. The Nazi official in Klagenfurt then ordered the lone remaining Jew to identify the bank accounts of all the departed Jews. Their money was withdrawn from these various accounts, and duly collected by the official. A deal was struck: in exchange for the money he obtained, he arranged for the release of all the Jews that had been transported to Dachau including, of course, Hermann. Frieda was, fortunately, already in Antwerp. Hermann was then able to reach Antwerp and join his wife. Amazingly, they were able to book a passage from Antwerp to the United States on one of the last German ships transporting Jews. The navy had been at odds with Hitler and had even previously signed a naval agreement with Great Britain.

Frieda's parents, at some point, were taken to a camp named Les Milles, which was located near Aix-en-Provence in the south of France. Although the camp was run with far less viciousness than the Nazi concentration camps, a considerable number of its inmates were eventually packed into railway wagons for deportation to Auschwitz. Frieda's father had an eye problem and was hidden by a Catholic ophthalmologist in a nearby eye hospital. The eye physician knew that this situation could not last long, and so arranged for them to stay with friends of his, the Donnier family, who hid them in their outhouse. Frieda's mother was a talented seamstress and was able to provide for her and her husband's well-being by making clothing for Madame Donnier.

In May 1939, a luxury liner, the St. Louis, set sail from Hamburg to Cuba. On board were 937 passengers, most of them Jewish refugees, including Frieda's parents who were seeking asylum from Nazi Germany. Captain Schroeder, in charge of the boat, went to great lengths to ensure dignified treatment for its Jewish passengers. Religious services were held in the dining room on Friday evenings, there were dances and concerts, and a bust of Hitler was covered with a tablecloth.

When the ship reached Havana, the Cuban government refused entry to all but 28 passengers. After five days, the St. Louis left Cuban waters and headed to Florida. Its passengers could clearly see the lights of Miami. The secretary of state, Cordell Hull, advised Franklin Roosevelt to deny permission to the passengers to disembark in the United States. After the St. Louis was turned away, a group of Canadians tried to persuade their prime minister to provide sanctuary to the passengers, but also to no avail. As Captain Schroder negotiated to find the passengers a safe haven, conditions on the ship declined. Very bravely, he refused to return the ship to Germany until all the passengers had been granted entry to some other country.

In the end, Great Britain, France, Belgium, and the Netherlands agreed to take all the refugees. While the vast majority sent to Britain survived, 30 percent of those returned to continental Europe were murdered during the Holocaust after the Nazis invaded these countries. Frieda's parents were allowed to return to Aix-en-Provence, where they stayed again with the Donniers and, under their protection, survived.

After the war, Hermann and Frieda stayed in touch with the Donniers. Because of the enormous risks they took hiding Frieda's parents, they were, like Mr. Glaser, the Swiss consul in Belgrade, eventually granted the title of "Righteous Gentiles" by Yad Vashem, the Holocaust Memorial Museum in Jerusalem. Captain Schroeder of the St. Louis was also named a Righteous Gentile. Both a book and a film, "Voyage of the Damned," were produced after the war, chronicling the fate of the doomed St. Louis.

Information about Joschi, the oldest of my mother's brothers, is rather scant because of his early death in the United States. We know that he went to the south of France, where he later found himself in a concentration camp. It is not clear if it was the same camp that housed Hermann, but it was run loosely enough that he was able to escape. Later, he was living underground in Belgrade and gave my father valuable advice for negotiating his rather complex situation there. Joschi was ultimately able to reach the United States, where he announced his intention to enlist in the U.S. Army. This helped him gain U.S. citizenship and, subsequently, to return to Europe in the Intelligence Service where he helped the Allies to identify Nazis.

On a side note, he managed to get himself photographed with Marlene Dietrich when she was entertaining the troops there. Joschi later met a charming lady named Ola Ilyanoski. They subsequently married and had a son, Steven, my only male cousin on my mother's side.

Edi also joined the U.S. Army. He took an intelligence test, came in first, and was immediately made an officer. In this capacity, he was sent to the Philippines where he contracted malaria. He was also in the first Army unit to land in Japan after the atomic bombs were dropped on Hiroshima and Nagasaki.

Back in the United States, Edi first lived with his father Jakob in New York City. He then moved to Bridgeport, Connecticut, where he opened a downtown hardware store which he ran with Hermann. When Edi joined the U.S. Army, Hermann and Frieda looked after the store. Hermann later went to night school to study law, and became a lawyer specializing in immigration issues.

Edi went to a hotel in the Catskill Mountains to help him recuperate from malaria. Sylvia was working at the front desk there. When she saw Edi entering the hotel, she told the other clerk, "I'll handle this guy's registration." Her daughter's guess, in retrospect, was that she must have thought him cute, despite the yellow tinge to his skin from the malaria medicine. When Edi was due to leave, he insisted that Sylvia depart with him, even though she was supposed to stay one more day on the job. He did not want to leave her behind in case she met anyone else! So, she left with Edi, and the rest, as they say, is history.

Edi and Sylvia had three daughters: Jessica, Sandy, and Miriam. Hermann and Frieda had two daughters: Susan and Evey. I subsequently became very good friends with all of these cousins. My wife Anne and I were fortunate enough to attend many weddings, bar mitzvahs and bat mitzvahs of these delightful relations in the northeast, and we have stayed in contact with them despite the distance that separates us. In this regard, I feel very blessed.

That almost all my family survived the Nazi's rise to power, and even prospered, is something for which I will always be grateful. These continuing relationships were particularly important to me because there was little contact with family members on my father's side until a much later time. Susan Schaier has always made a point to keep me informed of noteworthy Schaier events, which really helped when our meetings became less frequent. I'm very thankful for that.

The Onset of WWII and My Parents' Early Days in England

In September 1938, the Munich Agreement was signed by Neville Chamberlain, the British prime minister, and his French counterpart. In this infamous agreement, the Sudetenland, an area of Czechoslovakia that bordered Germany, was surrendered to Hitler, who was threatening to unleash a European war if an agreement could not be reached. Chamberlain arrived back in England waving a piece of paper that declared "Peace for our Time." Within a matter of days, the Sudetenland was invaded by German troops. The following year, on September 1, 1939, Hitler invaded Poland, and this led to the start of World War II, in which the Allies were to fight the two Axis powers, Germany and Italy.

With the declaration of war, my father was declared an "enemy alien" and was taken to Leeds Town Hall prison by Yank Appleson, who was a special police constable at the time. Yank was nearly reduced to tears as he carried out this unenviable duty. Afterwards, along with thousands of other Jews, including rabbis, my father was transferred to an internment camp at Huyton, Liverpool. This camp was in a new housing estate, where the accommodations were essentially devoid of any furniture. My mother, fortunately, was spared this indignity.

Many of these "enemy aliens" were Jewish refugees. It was, of course, most unlikely that Jewish "enemy aliens" would be sympathetic to the murderous Nazis. The internment camp was "home" to not only many Jews, but also communists, real Nazis, and even the grandson of Kaiser Wilhelm of Germany. My father appeared trustworthy and so was made an air raid warden. Existence there was remarkably boring, although he did learn to play bridge. He was later moved to another internment camp on the Isle of Man. Eventually, he was released and able to rejoin my mother in Leeds.

When later asked if he would help the war effort and enlist in the army, my father said that he would. However, this did not take place. Laci Fischer replied "no" to this question, as he was waiting to go to North America. Accordingly, Laci was put on the Arandora Star along with many Italians, German prisoners of war, and "enemy aliens" from internment camps. The ship was headed for Canada, but was mistaken for a battleship, torpedoed off the coast of Ireland, and sank with the loss of hundreds of lives. Laci, despite being overboard for several hours, managed to survive.

When my parents rejoined each other in Leeds, they first stayed with a very frumm (strictly orthodox) family, the Waldenbergs, who treated them very kindly. The only part of the house that was heated was the kitchen, and my parents' bedroom windows were always kept open. Sleep, therefore, required several heavy pullovers. At this time, my father had not yet obtained a work permit, so he was unable to go to the Applesons' shoe factory. My parents moved to several other shared or rented locations, so it was quite some time before they finally acquired their first home. At some point in this new home, the three crates from Vienna that the Hungarian accountant had taken to the United States arrived unexpectedly on their doorstep.

When my father was finally able to work, he found that, while the shoe factory machinery was up to date, almost no one there knew how to use it. It took almost two years before my father was able to establish a fully functional system of operation. As time went by, my father introduced Applesons' shoes to new customers and was also offered positions with other companies, including the well-known chain of Marks and Spencer. However, he decided to stay at Applesons. Although my father had learned some English in Vienna, he had not yet achieved fluency in this foreign tongue. He had a hard time understanding the Yorkshire accent and carried a dictionary with him day and night. My parents often went to the cinema, where they learned far more English than from any of the lessons they attended.

After the war ended, Applesons started exporting to many countries including Switzerland, Iceland, Egypt, and members of the Commonwealth. According to the Shoe Manufacturer's Federation, the company was apparently the second-largest exporter of shoes in the country. My father visited Japan, partly because cheap shoes from the Far East were threatening the shoe industry in Great Britain. He was fascinated by the entirely different culture that he experienced while there. He also went to Israel, where he spent time with his younger brother Hans. They discussed setting up a factory in Israel, but ultimately decided against this. While there, he bought a plot of land which he later gave to Hans.

There is no doubt that my father had a strong determination and will to succeed. I think this probably came from my grandfather who, after all, had spent a lifetime establishing a shoe business starting essentially from scratch. He was unhesitatingly honest and earned other people's respect because of this untarnished quality. As was clear from his escape from Austria, he needed to be resilient in order to overcome enormous odds. He took his work very seriously and was always looking for opportunities to lead the firm's business in new directions. As his status in the Applesons' shoe factory rose, he eventually became its managing director. He was, nevertheless, always modest about his achievements.

Reflections on My Family's Background

It is interesting to look back on my father's and mother's family. Both of their parents came from a relatively poor background. My father's grandfather owned a pub in a small village of Slovakia, and my mother's grandfather came from Galicia, an impoverished region of Poland. Both these locations were outposts of the once mighty Habsburg Empire.

My paternal grandfather somehow made it to Vienna, the empire's illustrious capital, and my maternal grandfather found his way to Klagenfurt which, if not possessing the grandeur of Vienna, was at least a provincial capital. Both built businesses from scratch, my paternal grandfather establishing a shoe factory and my maternal grandfather a department store and, later, a shoe store. All were clearly successful enterprises, which must have entailed a great deal of dedication and hard work. A side benefit was that the shoe business facilitated the relationship between my parents, since my mother made many trips to Vienna to buy shoes from my grandfather's shoe factory there. Life, at least with respect to their material existence, was a happy one until antisemitism reared its ugly head. Perhaps this happiness led my parents to hang on to that existence for far too long. They moved into a beautiful apartment in Vienna in 1936 when, clearly, the writing was already on the wall. But, it is easy for me to say this in retrospect, for I was not there at the time.

Part Two
CHILDHOOD YEARS IN LEEDS

My Earliest Years

Understandably, my parents had no desire to bring any child of theirs into existence until it was very clear that the Allies were winning the war. They had no interest whatsoever in a repeat performance of their tortuous escape from Austria. And so it was that I did not arrive on the scene in Leeds until May 9, 1943. Curiously, at the time of my conception, the Allies had not yet gained the upper hand in the war. The turning point would only come when the Germans suffered catastrophic losses in the battle for Stalingrad in November of that year. Maybe I was an accident, or maybe my parents had a crystal ball that could predict the future. Either way, I was here and, hopefully, here to stay.

I was a highly prized only child, as I was later to find out, because my mother had been diagnosed with both mitral stenosis and hypertension, which had made her pregnancy a difficult one. She had been told that it was unsafe for her to risk bearing a second child. Despite these health issues, I do not remember her being handicapped by breathlessness or limitations on the distance that she was able to walk.

My very first memories are of a visit to Switzerland when I was five years old. Because of recurring sinus problems, I was whisked off by my parents to the resort of Villars, about two hours from Geneva, in the hope that its pure mountain air would open my nasal passages. While Villars itself was, I am told, a beautiful place, what I remember most were rather disturbing experiences. Once, on the occasion of a bath in the hotel, I suddenly deposited a large chunk of stool on the side of the tub. Since I was now five, this was both unexpected and highly embarrassing.

Far worse were the instructions from a nurse to lie on the bed on my stomach. I soon came to know what this heralded. It was the entry of a huge steel needle, connected to a tube of penicillin, that was rammed deeply into whatever meager muscles were gathered around my rear end. Needless to say, I increasingly dreaded each repetition of this process. Surprisingly, these frequent invasions of my buttocks did not appear to improve the state of my sinuses, for the problem continued unabated.

In Leeds, my parents and I lived at 46, Wyncliffe Gardens, a modest semi-detached house in Moortown. I have no memories of the county primary school that I attended there, probably because the teaching was unremarkable. The building adjacent to the school housed the conservative synagogue to which my parents belonged, although my father was quite scathing about this traditional temple of prayer and joined the newer, more approachable Jewish Reform synagogue. I do not, however, remember him attending services there.

Nevertheless, probably because of my mother's insistence, I was expected to attend the Hebrew evening school, or Cheder, next door to my day school. Before long, it became clear that I was woefully inadequate at learning to read Hebrew and, far worse, had very little idea what the words meant. I did not see how all the required effort served any useful purpose. It seemed ridiculous to spend so much time attempting to master material that I perceived as arcane, and so I started to play truant from these classes as often as possible. Subsequently, when my bar mitzvah loomed, I would pay quite a price for these frequent absences. As I look back, this was clearly the start of my dissatisfaction with the Jewish religion. I was already following in my father's footsteps.

When I was nine, I was transferred to the junior school of Leeds Grammar School (LGS). Unlike my previous school, this was a private, tuition-paying school. We all wore smart looking navy blazers to which the school's crest was attached. Perhaps because of this, we were often referred to, tongue in cheek, as "grammar grubs."

On my first day of school there, the class master went through the list of students alphabetically. My overriding memory of this was related to a pupil named Baird. It was not his last name that fascinated me, but rather that he was introduced to the class as J.A.W.D.C. Baird. I did not know that it was possible to have so many first and middle names and assumed this indicated that he came from a family of considerable pedigree and distinction. It was a shock to hear his name called out, together with the preceding initials, as it suggested that England quietly boasted of a strong class system to which I clearly did not belong.

I do not remember any of my teachers at LGS, but I still have my report cards. In my first term there, my form master commented: "Talks too much and is too fussy over trifles." Another stain on my sheet was the house master's comment: "Cannot swim," which was to become a familiar refrain over the next two years. This must have been particularly upsetting to my father who, you will remember, was a truly excellent swimmer. It was not until I was 11 or 12 that I conquered my fear of water and learned to swim. By that time, everyone else in the class was easily lapping me in the pool.

My two years in junior school indicated that I was a very good pupil in geography, history, and French, a trait passed down to me by my father, but an abysmal performer in physics and mathematics. For the latter two subjects, I was near the very bottom of my class. In the second year of junior school, we started to learn Latin. In days gone by, knowledge of Latin was considered essential if one wanted to pursue a career in medicine, but this was, fortunately, no longer the case.

As a mollycoddled only child who had arrived relatively late in my parents' life (my father was already 38), there was no doubt that I was considerably spoiled. While most Jewish children that I knew were spoiled, this applied even more so if you were the only offspring. My parents essentially catered to all my needs and were overly inclined to praise me at every opportunity. They also would frequently remind me to "be careful." I took this to mean that any physical risk should be avoided. It also made sense, because I was a skinny kid and intuitively lacked even a smidgen of bravery.

My parents, being classical music devotees, arranged for me to take piano lessons. Almost all the Jewish children of European refugees were expected to play the piano, because classical music was a mainstay of our culture. After two or so years, my piano teacher suddenly expected me to make a big keyboard jump into, I believe, some music of Chopin. This did not sit well with me on the piano stool, and, to the teacher's considerable surprise, I promptly gave notice. Following my abrupt departure, I never again played the piano.

First Friendships

My friends at the time came in two flavors: non-Jewish and Jewish. These two groups were like oil and water, for they did not mix. The friends on my street were non-Jewish. A girl of about my age, Anne Lauderdale, lived next door and we often played together, although I have no recollection at what we played. Christopher Davidson lived a few doors away and, with him, I played street cricket using lamp posts as wickets.

Cricket was big in those days. Intensely boring five-day international test matches, including Sundays as a mandatory day of rest, were all the rage. My favorite player was a dashing, stylish character named Dennis Compton. He was not quite up to the standard of Len Hutton, one of the world's best batsmen who hailed from Pudsey, a town only 15 or so miles from Leeds, but Len, like many other Yorkshiremen, was far too dour for my taste.

My parent's friends, without exception, were Jewish. There was nothing dour about those who, like my parents, were refugees from Nazi-occupied Europe. Many were colorful characters, and had no problem expressing themselves, despite oftentimes doing so with a broken accent. Naturally, as a youngster, I became friendly with some of their children. The closest of our friends during this time were the Denton family, even though their children, James and Janet, attended a different school. Their mother, Margit, was a charming, dominating and slightly aristocratic lady who was a refugee from Sofia, Bulgaria. Our two families shared many highly enjoyable times together.

Other friends came about through school and, although we did not know their parents, they were almost invariably Jewish. One of these, Michael Cooke, who was affectionately known as Cookie, had a puckish sense of humor. Michael was friends with a girl named Sonya Segal. It was her father, Sam Segal, who later arranged an exhibition match in Leeds featuring Pancho Gonzalez and Pancho Segura, two world renowned tennis players. Pancho Gonzalez was the world's best tennis player for several years and had already become an idol of mine. I would practice his serve many a time until both I and the racket were ready to drop.

Since most of my relatives had escaped to the United States, we had little family in England and no family whatsoever in Leeds. There was no adherence to any traditional Jewish ritual in our household. My mother was relatively religious but was overpowered by my father's rejection of both God and the Jewish religion. I did experience, from time to time, Sabbath evening prayer and dinners at the home of friends of ours. Joining these warm family occasions was delightful and filled a gap in my home life, which was devoid of any ritual.

Improving Circumstances and Travel Home and Abroad

My father came to England in 1938 as a designer for the Appleson shoe factory. Yank and Ike Appleson were the brothers who ran the factory. Sadly, Yank, who I remember as a very outgoing, jolly character, became an alcoholic. As this progressed, he became less and less able to handle responsibility. Even more tragically, Yank also suffered from schizophrenia. Eventually, he succumbed to the combined effects of these disorders. My father was not enamored with Ike at all. He would comment that Ike was well suited to tying string around the shoe boxes, but little else. Diplomacy, I should mention, was never a major suite in my father's hand. He was unsparing in his commitment to the company, and he expected the same from those who worked in the factory.

The demanding responsibilities of running and growing the firm's shoe business took its toll on my father. While the company's fortunes were on the upswing, there was a price to pay for there were many evenings when, after dinner, my father would flop into his favorite armchair and fall fast asleep. I vowed never to flog myself that hard, but nevertheless later found myself frequently working unrestrainedly in a similarly unbalanced way. Juggling the demands of work while paying sufficient attention to life's other needs is never an easy task, especially in the early stages of one's career.

As England was beginning to recover from the devastation caused by the war, a gradual improvement in both the economy and the country's infrastructure took place. At one point, Prime Minister Harold MacMillan famously informed the country: "You've never had it so good." Unfortunately, this could not be said for his private life since, for many years, he meekly tolerated his wife's highly publicized affair with Robert Boothby, one of the backbenchers in his own party. While Great Britain's aristocratic leader exhibited a stiff upper lip in public, his private life was a complete shambles.

A favorite annual destination of ours in May, when the weather was starting to improve, was Grasmere in the Lake District. We would stay there in a hotel that had an enviable location overlooking the lake deep in the heart of tranquil Wordsworth countryside. I can still visualize myself rowing on the lake and, skinny as I was, needing help from my father to ensure that the boat kept moving forward.

We also made sporadic visits to the Yorkshire coast, which was within easy reach. I vaguely remember several trips to Scarborough, a popular seaside town that boasted a long beach complete with a pier, excellent fish and chips, and much more. Back in those days, as was customary in most parts of Yorkshire, the fish and chips were usually eaten out of the local newspaper. You had no choice of newspaper. You either grabbed the food with ever more greasy fingers or left the tasty morsels swimming in the paper's headlines.

When I was older, we would sometimes venture to nearby Filey, the main attraction of which for me was the pitch and putt, or par three, golf course. This was my introduction to the demanding game of golf, which was later to consume much of my spare time. Subsequently, as my father's business interests flourished, we were able to vacation in Devon on England's south coast, and even travelled to northern France and Switzerland.

My mother had not seen her three brothers, Edi, Hermann, and Joschi, since their hasty escape from Austria in 1938. All three had made their way to the American northeast while my parents had landed, and stayed, in England. After such a long interval, she was naturally anxious to see them again. So it was that in 1953, when I was 10 years old, my mother and I made an eagerly awaited trip to the United States to stay with my uncles and their families for several weeks.

We traveled to the United States on two famed transatlantic cruise ships: the Queen Elizabeth for the outward journey and the Queen Mary for our return home. These floating hotels carrying up to 2,000 passengers were still in their heyday. The first non-stop transatlantic jet flights did not take place until five years later, in 1958. The crossing took five days which, for a 10-year-old, were five days filled with awe and excitement. Every day, we would receive a wide-ranging list of children's activities from which I could choose. I was suddenly living in a fantasy world, far removed from my relatively humdrum existence in Leeds. To further heighten the excitement, I managed to sneak into the first-class section of the ship on several occasions, the elegance of which was even more amazing. I think that this was the beginning of my enduring fascination with the lifestyle of the "rich and famous."

I was enthralled by New York City, never having seen anything remotely like it. Joschi lived literally underneath the George Washington Bridge. His son Steven was the only cousin close to my age, so we played a variety of games together. The other cousins were either far too young, or not yet born. My other two uncles lived in Connecticut. Edi's home was in Bridgeport, and Hermann lived in Fairfield. This is when I first met my Aunt Sylvia, who would later be so helpful in telling me about my mother's family.

Major Changes:
A Different School and a Different Address

At the age of 11, we were required to take a pernicious examination called the Eleven Plus. This was a crucial test, for it determined whether I could go to a grammar school, where I would be prepared for university. Those who failed were consigned to attend a technical or secondary modern school, with little to no chance of going on to university, instead being instructed on how to learn a trade. In retrospect, it was patently absurd that a single examination taken at the tender age of 11 would have so much influence on one's future career.

The pass rate of the Eleven Plus was around 20 percent, so the odds were stacked against most of the 11-year-old pupils. However, among all my Jewish friends, I only knew of one who failed this examination. Our parents repeatedly emphasized the importance of academic success, so a huge stigma lay over this hapless student's head. Academic prowess was particularly expected of children born to refugee parents like mine, many of whom had owned businesses in central Europe. These parents stressed that it had been well near impossible to take any of their businesses with them when they were forced to flee. It was made abundantly clear to us that we should learn a profession that we could carry with us if yet another catastrophe was to befall us Jews. Since the law of the land varied from country to country, a career in medicine was considered a more transportable option than one in law.

Like virtually all my friends, I cleared this absurd Eleven Plus hurdle with apparent ease. I now had the choice of transferring to a public secondary grammar school, or staying at the private, tuition-paying LGS. My parents were convinced that the future lay in science, and that science was clearly better taught at Roundhay Grammar School (RGS), which was a public school. I was very upset at the idea of transferring to RGS, especially since most of my friends attended LGS. But, following my parents' strong insistence, I acquiesced and moved on to what was very unfamiliar territory.

The following year, when I was 12, a momentous change of address took place. We moved up the hill, both literally and metaphorically, from Moortown to Alwoodley. In those days, there was a distinct pattern of migration from Chapeltown to Moortown and then to Alwoodley, if at all economically feasible. Chapeltown was once the most exclusive part of the inner city but as businesses moved into that part of the city, the businessmen who lived there started to move their families to the leafy suburbs of Alwoodley and Roundhay. Moortown occupied somewhat of a middle ground. In the 40 or so years since I left, Chapeltown had become the scene of both riots and deadly gang warfare related to drug smuggling. This was not the case when I was a child. I well remember Chapeltown's marvelous public library, where one of my parents would often drop me off for the entire day. There, I spent many happy hours in a literary haven perusing a wide variety of books. In recent years, fortunately, Chapeltown has regained some of its past vigor and community spirit.

Alwoodley was a totally different environment compared to Moortown. There was, as already implied, manifestly greater wealth in this furthest north suburb of Leeds. As evidence of this, the houses were considerably larger and often sported attractive gardens. We moved into a detached house at 36, Sandhill Oval. Because of the high concentration of Jewish people in Alwoodley, it was sometimes referred to, in a clearly derogatory way, as "All-yid-ley." I well remember a non-Jewish family that moved into the house immediately opposite us in Sandhill Oval. Little did they know that they had unwittingly entered a Jewish enclave. After two or three years in their new house, they decided to move elsewhere. It would have been quite impertinent for me to enquire what was the reasoning behind this move, but I can certainly hazard a guess.

I made friends with some of my classmates at RGS but, true to the pattern of my earlier life, they were almost all Jewish. There was only one exception: Richard Stapleton, the son of our butcher in Moortown. Richard filled a very useful role, for he was an extremely good cricket player. We had a recreation ground close to our home in Sandhill Oval, and there we would engage in a somewhat serious version of the sport. We also used this recreation ground for soccer games which were often vigorously contested, so much so that one of my friends suffered a broken leg after being tackled.

In our new location, I rapidly made good friends with neighborhood boys of my age. All went to LGS, and all were Jewish. During the colder weather, we would frequently indulge in Monopoly and Totopoly (the latter a horse-racing board game). Monopoly had a particular appeal as it was heavily based on accumulating money and involved the purchase of properties of varying status and cost. We were a close-knit group and had much fun playing sports on the recreation ground and these indoor board games in the winter.

At RGS, despite the supposedly strong teaching of science there, I continued to be lamentably weak in both physics and mathematics. The latter posed a particular problem. If one wished to study the sciences in high school at RGS, it was mandatory to obtain a pass at Ordinary Level (O Level) in mathematics. Since I was so pathetic at this subject, my parents set me up with a private tutor, Mr. Glick, to improve my ability to comprehend its many complexities. I remember him as an excellent teacher who was very encouraging in boosting my confidence at understanding this alien subject. He taught me how to believe in myself and that I was able to make progress even when the slope seemed too steep.

I continued to perform strongly in history and geography, as well as English language and English literature. French was an additional subject, and in this I also showed considerable proficiency. Our French teacher was a monstrous fellow named Mr. Ferguson, whose blatant antisemitism was well known. On one test, I submitted an essay in French to him. To my amazement, he gave me a mark of one out of 40. I asked him why I did so poorly. His preposterous reply was that it represented a charity mark. My masters' end-of-term reports, as was the case at LGS, remained rather mixed in their comments. Disturbingly, more than one of my masters stated in writing that I needed to think more before opening my mouth.

I do not know, even now, that I have shown much improvement in this regard.

Supplementary classes included swimming and gym. I have already covered my inadequacies related to swimming, but now I also had to contend with gym. For one of our gym activities, we were expected to vault lengthwise over a pommel horse without bars. This involved running up to the horse, and then leaping high enough to clear its entire length. Clearly, after placing one's hands on the horse, the next anatomical parts that could potentially hit this loathsome object were your testicles. Accordingly, I obstinately hung at the end of the line and never once attempted the maneuver, for castration was not part of my life's game plan.

This lack of heroism extended to rugby, which initially was a mandatory sport. If anyone was indeed foolish enough to pass the ball to me, I would immediately throw it to a teammate. There was one occasion, however, when no teammate was anywhere near me, and I had no choice but to run for the touchline. I avoided a tackle only by deliberately and clumsily running into the waiting defensive opponent. When we were given the opportunity to switch from rugby to cross-country running, my arm shot up immediately in favor of the latter.

Surviving My Bar Mitzvah

I was now attending the conservative synagogue in Moortown on a fairly regular basis, spurred on by both my forthcoming bar mitzvah and my newly made observant friends in our neighborhood. In accordance with the temple's conservative nature, congregants usually walked to the temple, which was more than a mile away. This unnecessary exercise did not appeal to me, so I usually took the bus there. I took care to alight one stop before the temple, so I could be perceived as "playing ball."

What took place in the temple was hardly inspirational. The women, by the way, were seated upstairs and therefore out of sight, but not necessarily out of mind. The men fell into two categories. There were those who were praying almost uninterruptedly, and as they did so rocked their bodies back and forth in a movement often referred to as "davening," and those who adopted a far different approach. For the latter, attending the synagogue was an opportunity to discuss not only business but also the soccer game that our cherished local team, Leeds United, would be playing that afternoon. Some, of course, blatantly violated the conservative approach to the sabbath by attending the game. Who said religious practice needed meticulous observation?

Almost every Jewish boy that I knew went through the solemn preparation required for their bar mitzvah. This ceremony and training at the age of 13 years is meant to ensure that the commandments will, from then on, be obeyed and that the recipient will become a responsible adult. There were few bat mitzvahs in those days. It was not until the 1970s that this practice was made widely available to girls.

Preparation for one's bar mitzvah was no piece of cake. It required much study, understanding, and the ability to chant the appropriate part of the Torah. My reading of Hebrew script was at best marginal because of my truancy in earlier years. Furthermore, I had a terrible singing voice. Somehow, though, I managed to get my act together in readiness for the dreaded occasion and stumbled through the required chanting of the text. I think the rabbi came to my rescue more than a few times during this process.

There was the usual bar mitzvah party later in the day. I have no recollection whatsoever of this, but I do know that I adamantly refused to give the customary speech. I was far too nervous, and probably was still suffering residual shock after my morning ordeal in the synagogue. However, I remember a bevy of presents, especially the receipt of approximately six Parker pens and an almost similar number of Sheaffer pens. Fortunately, a large number of book tokens compensated for these essentially unwanted gifts.

After the bar mitzvah, I started the accepted practice of wrapping tefillin. These are small leather boxes which are strapped around the head and arm and contain passages from the Torah. I dutifully carried this out for a year or more, and then concluded that, for me, it provided little or, more truthfully, no spiritual benefit. This marked the beginning of my de-acclimatization from Jewish rituals, which had clearly been tenuous in the best of times. Halting this black box practice was undoubtedly influenced by my irreligious father, who felt it served no purpose whatsoever.

Life Beyond School

In my early teens, I became increasingly interested in playing golf. My golf was played on a nine-hole municipal course in Roundhay. Two new friends, Bernard Olsburgh and Ashley Levi, often joined me to make a small, but determined, threesome. One of the beauties of this course was the closeness of the sixth green to the first tee. Especially when playing alone, if I was dissatisfied with my score over the initial five holes, I would return to the first tee and repeat the process, if necessary four or even five times.

I had many enjoyable rounds of golf on this nine-hole course and fell in love with the sport. Golf had become a strong preoccupation, and I was to play many, many rounds in the forthcoming years. The game is really a microcosm of life: it is you against the course and anything else is quite irrelevant. If you want to learn about someone's true character, watch how they handle themselves on the golf course and how they reveal themselves after one or two drinks. It is that simple!

There was a predominantly Jewish golf club in Leeds named Moor Allerton of which my father was an intermittent tennis member. He felt the club was filled with nouveaux riche who were demonstrably proud of themselves, and perhaps he was right. The club was formed in the 1920s in direct response to the policy of many nearby major golf clubs to refuse admission to Jews. This was particularly true of the most prestigious of these clubs, Moortown, which actually objected to the building of Moor Allerton.

I had a friend named Doug Curry with whom I golfed from time to time at Roundhay. One day, Doug invited me to play at Moortown. I was thrilled at the prospect of playing this historic course, even though its membership still did not admit Jews. Later that week, Doug shamefacedly informed me that I, even as a guest, would be unable to play there. I knew the reason, and did not want to embarrass him, so I immediately dropped the subject. Years later, I got some revenge, albeit limited. Our house was only five or ten minutes from the course, so I would sometimes sneak out onto the course and pocket as many balls as possible. I was detected only once, and then professed ignorance as to my ploy on their private property. I was curtly asked to leave, but I had already scooped up a fair number of their gentile balls. Sweet, sweet revenge! Throughout the remainder of my life, I was to find considerable pleasure and excitement in trespassing in all manner of locations.

I also played a lot of tennis, often with James Denton or Michael Cooke. Both were much better players than I, but they put up with my limited attempts to give them a good game. Sometimes Pancho Gonzales' serve worked, but usually not. I enrolled to play in some local youth tennis tournaments, either with Hilary Lyons, the sister of one of my neighborhood friends John Lyons, or with James Denton. I was under no illusion that we would progress in any of the few tournaments that we entered, but we had a good time trying our best. In school cricket, I was a reasonable batsman for a while and played intramural cricket on several occasions. However, wearing glasses and facing increasingly fast bowling started to make me nervous, and my ability to wield the bat with any success thereafter declined.

On the backside of our garden, if you hopped over the wall, there were fields stretching for quite a distance. I had decided to become a javelin thrower, in the hope that I could have some success on the school's annual sports day if I persevered. So, I constructed a javelin out of bamboo poles, adding a sharp point at one end to encourage this object to stick into the ground. Despite my lack of muscle, I practiced hard but, alas, to no avail when push came to shove.

Chess: The Go-To Board Game that Connected me to Friends

Most kids at RGS played a "soft version" of rugby during the lunch break called "touch and pass." It was played on concrete, which was not exactly the softest of surfaces. I turned, instead, to the indoor game of chess. Historically, chess provided a replacement for the violent struggle of warfare with a calmer, nonviolent competition that was a battle of the minds, hence the presence of kings, queens, knights, castles, and bishops on the chess board. The pawns, of course, were mere foot soldiers. Anyway, substituting chess for the physically aggressive game of real rugby seemed a good idea.

The chess club was decidedly short of participants, for chess was not considered a very manly sport. As I improved, I started to play on the school's chess team. I had become very friendly with Bernard Olsburgh, who was always a far better player. I think that this encouraged me to try to improve. Chess openings were a complete mystery. How could anyone possibly learn all the variations for each of the many openings? Nevertheless, I played as the fourth, or occasionally third, player on the six-man team. I made my moves as slowly as the clock would allow, so I was usually good for a draw. Accordingly, wins were rather rare!

For the next several decades, I did not play the game. After retiring, I joined a group of players in a very informal, nearby club. When I was beaten by a 12-year-old, and then even by a nine-year-old, I decided it was time to quit. These kids would wander around to observe other games in progress, or even play other games simultaneously, while I scratched my head in vain. There is a limit to how foolish one can look, and I had clearly reached that point.

Two or three years ago, a friend of mine, Irwin Labin, mentioned that he was a keen player, so I decided to play him, and occasionally a few others, in an on-line chess club, Chess.com. Irwin nearly always beats me, and he tells me to play more against other folks to gain experience. Well, maybe, maybe…next winter. We will see. I love the game, despite still not knowing the openings and making at least two or three "blunders" per game, according to Chess.com. Every game is different, and you never know what stunts your opponent will try to pull on you, so every game is, believe it or not, a thrill.

Decades later, Bernard and I reconnected and became good friends. He made Aliyah (migrated) to Israel and we made a point of staying in touch. He had been a family doctor and had developed a special role towards the end of his career supervising and training future generations of colleagues. Another friend, John Dyson, who had been in the same class as me at LGS, played chess for that school but I do not remember playing against him in any of the matches.

John went on to become a barrister, then a judge, then a Supreme Court judge, when he acquired the title of Lord, and finally became Master of the Rolls, the second-highest position for a lawyer in England. It was Bernard who told me of John's brilliantly written autobiography, "A Judge's Journey," which strongly influenced me to attempt this work. Sometimes a push is needed to embark on such a task, and I will always recognize the encouragement it gave me. Today, revising this very page of the draft, I received an email from John informing me that he had been diagnosed with hairy cell leukemia. I was shocked to the core and close to tears.

Losing My Mother and Moving Forward

I remember well a wonderful holiday with my parents in North Wales, which I found fascinating. There was, among other sights, the splendid Conway Castle, as it was known to the English. Its real name, though, in Welsh, was Conwy Castle. We also visited a charming seaside village named Portmeirion, which had been built in the manner of an Italian village. Since I had not yet been to Italy, it felt to me like a fantasyland, which was the architect's intention. On numerous occasions, it has been the location for film and television productions.

During that trip in the summer of 1957, I started taking photographs for the first time. My camera was the very popular Kodak Brownie, a camera which dated back to 1900, at which time it was no more than a black cardboard box to which a simple lens was attached. Thanks to this Brownie, it was the only family trip on which I took quite a few photographs of my mother and father.

In early 1958, my mother suddenly died. The cause was mitral stenosis and hypertension. In those days, surgery for mitral stenosis was very crude and she was not considered a suitable candidate for such a risky operation. She was only 46 years old. I was stunned and my father was distraught unlike I had ever seen him before. Accordingly, I felt the need to be of help to him and to be more grown up than was normal for a boy 14 years of age. My good friend James Denton remembers me calling him to calmly say that I could not play tennis in a local competition that day because my mother had just died. Maybe I was just trying to be calm on the surface.

My reaction to this abrupt shock was one of total denial. To this very day, I do not remember going through any period of grieving. I will never understand why this was the case. What I do know, however, is that memories of my mother and our family life before her death then became very scant. How I wish I could remember her better. I knew that her friends regarded her highly, and that she contributed considerable time to helping Jewish charitable organizations. But where did all those other memories go? Memories that would have reflected her goodness, her dignity, and her love for both my father and me. That is something I will never know. Those recent photographs of us from North Wales, though scant compensation, offered some sweet memories.

Following our huge loss, my father and I had a succession of housekeepers who cooked and kept our house in order. One of the early domestic aides was a highly attractive, young au pair girl from France. While she was reasonably competent in carrying out her tasks, it was nakedly obvious that she went out many evenings only to arrive back from these forays in the early hours of the morning. After a few months, she contracted a sexually transmitted disease. When she professed ignorance as to how this could have happened, my father caustically opined that she may have become infected by watching too much television. Another housekeeper insisted on eating dinner with us, which dampened any meaningful conversation between my father and myself. Unsurprisingly, she was also soon gone. We eventually hired a long-tenured housekeeper, Mrs. Cockerham, who bore an unmistakable resemblance to a fierce bulldog. There was nothing subtle about her, not in her conversation, her attitude, or her appearance.

At this stage of my life, I enjoyed going to numerous parties for the well-heeled Jewish lads and lasses of Alwoodley, some of which were rather fancy affairs. Dancing was a critical way to become acquainted with any of the girls who caught your fancy at these parties. Unfortunately, an abiding and lifelong failing of mine was the complete inability to feel any rhythm whatsoever when attempting to dance. Naturally, out of profound embarrassment, I would abstain from asking anyone of the opposite sex to cut the rug with me. I have never really conquered this fear of dancing, and I continually watch my feet instead of

All dressed up, aged five

Great uncle Benno, who saved my parents' lives

My mother and me, Wales 1957

Time for long trousers

looking at my partner. This, of course, did nothing in my teen years to encourage even the slightest hint of bonding. All I could do was look on enviously as my friends glided in tune to the music with apparent ease and in all directions.

Is "All the World a Stage on which all the Men and Women are Merely Players?"

For some, the stage can be a daunting experience. For others, their lives, so to speak, may consist entirely of a one-act play. I suspect that most of us fall somewhere between these two extremes. It is still not entirely clear where I stand in this regard but, with many opportunities to appear on stage in later life, it seemed that I was able to overcome any initial fears.

My first experience on the stage was hardly a success, for it took place on the podium where I recited the required piece of the Torah for my bar mitzvah. As you will remember, this unhinged me so much that I declined to give a speech on a different stage at my bar mitzvah party that evening. Two performances in one day at that tender age were clearly not in the cards.

The next stage on which I was slated to appear was the annual school play, when I was about 15 years old. The play was "The Miser," by Moliere. I had landed, to my surprise, a large role. The part I played was Cleante, who was an ardent suitor of a young dame named Mariane. This was problematic, for the school had only male students. To make matters worse, Mariane was played by the cantor's son, David Apfel, with whom I was friendly, but not that friendly. At one point during rehearsal, I had to deliver some passionate lines, and here I paraphrase: "Ah, her nose, her lips, her cheeks etc. etc." which I uttered entirely devoid of any feeling. The drama teacher immediately stopped proceedings as I attempted this exultation about the uppermost parts of Mariane's body, dressed in drag as he (she) was. "Kohut (for that was my name at the time)," he exclaimed, "Have you never been in love?" That was a tough nut to crack, for my mother had passed away two years previously, and I had not yet moved on to any amorous relationships. "No," I replied truthfully. Furthermore, it did not help that I moved about the stage like a clumsy bulldozer.

When my father saw the show, he offered his verdict. Keep in mind that I was a precious only Jewish son, and so I was not accustomed to being dismissed as incapable. "Freddie," he declared, "You are no actor." My overinflated balloon had been summarily pricked. My father's statement proved to be prophetically true for, each year, my roles progressively shrank. In my final stage appearance, I was given a non-speaking part in which all that was required of me was to offer drinks, wordlessly, from a tray to assorted guests. I can report that I managed to avoid spilling the drinks. Although a miserly role, I was very relieved to be let off so lightly.

Like Many Others, a Confused Teenager

The next few years saw some major changes in my life. Moving to a public school, RGS, had been decidedly traumatic, for I had entered an unfamiliar environment that was far less privileged than the one to which I had grown accustomed. I now recognize that this move signaled my entrance into the real world and that this was a world that I needed to understand. Since I had to adapt at some point in my life, it was perhaps a good idea to "get on with it" now. Nevertheless, it seemed a contradiction that when we moved "up the hill" to Alwoodley, I was now at RGS while all my new friends went to the private school, LGS. I had a hard time making sense of this, especially as Jewish families placed such a high premium on education and I appeared to be bucking this trend. That I was bullied a bit between classes did not help, but it was never vicious and so I could absorb it.

And now my mind is blocked, as I come to the loss of my mother which so dramatically changed my world. To get through this block, as I push myself to type, I am listening to the Adagietto from Mahler's Fifth Symphony, as poignant a piece as was ever written. I wonder how my emotions and my relationships might have been different if my mother had been there during my formative teen years. There were some awkward times that arose with the opposite sex, and I had no guidance as to how to handle them. You cannot run a race unless your feet are in the starting blocks. My father's shoe business might have helped, but it was not into manufacturing running shoes.

Our housekeepers were utterly devoid of any sensitivity, and managing teenage issues was not part of their job description anyway. My father had always been strong and resolute, but the loss of my mother made him almost inconsolable. He once told me that, if it was not for my existence, he would have driven his car off a cliff. He usually hid his emotions, but they came to the forefront when he lost his mother and mother-in-law and now, even more so, with the loss of his wife. It fell to me to carry him through the terrible times he now faced, and this responsibility may have contributed to the denial and suppression of so much of our family life that we had previously enjoyed.

As I advanced through middle school, my father and godfather, Joe Overton, discussed possible careers with me. Their suggestions were limited to just four professions; medicine, dentistry, law, or accountancy, which, as already mentioned, were based on the ability to take any acquired professional knowledge to another country if forced to flee. My father and godfather, who was both wise and pragmatic, made these limited choices abundantly clear to me.

At about this time, I read "The Citadel," a novel by A.J. Cronin about an idealist family doctor in Wales. Unquestionably, this fueled my desire to become a doctor despite my continued mediocrity in all the science subjects. There was no logic whatsoever behind this choice. It was my intention to become a psychiatrist. My father's Viennese background and my superficial understanding of psychoanalysis, a subject that had clearly fascinated my father, probably contributed to this future goal. Additionally, my mother's death likely made me more aware of matters related to the mind than those related to the body.

In retrospect, it was clear that law would have been a far, far better option for me, especially as I had acquired the gift of the gab (sometimes more than needed) and could express myself clearly in writing. I even contemplated going to law school when I was in my forties but realized that was not going to put bread on the table for Anne, me, and our young family. You may well ask why we were making decisions about the direction of our long-term future at the tender age of 16, but that was how the system worked in those days.

Middle School: Time to Make Choices

I found few of the classes in middle school to be exciting. There were, admittedly, some exceptions. In history, we studied Europe going forwards from the French Revolution. This was an opportunity to learn about many gripping French, English, and German battles, conquests, and, in the case of France, a bevy of quick executions. However, all of this was ultimately transformed into a mere memory test. In English literature, we examined Shakespeare's "Julius Caesar" in considerable detail. I found the villain Cassius, and the more upstanding Brutus, so easily misled by Cassius, to be a fascinating pair of characters. My recall of what we studied in the other seven subjects that constituted my "O" (Ordinary Level) examinations is limited. Newton's Law of Gravity and grave trigonometric issues were probably somewhere in there, but my memories of them lie conveniently suppressed.

The results of these examinations mattered greatly, as they determined which three subjects we could choose for our two years of high school. The basic decision was, of course, between the arts and the sciences. Science required "O" level passes in physics, chemistry, and mathematics, which I somehow managed to achieve. All in all, I passed eight of the nine "O" level examinations, failing, to my complete surprise, English literature, which was one of my stronger subjects. Looking back on the critical essay in this examination, I attributed everything Brutus said to the cunning, manipulative Cassius, whereas I hitched onto Cassius all the noble qualities of Brutus. Clearly, this major mixup accounted for my miserable performance in this subject.

Three high school subjects needed to be selected. With the goal of becoming a doctor, I decided on physics, chemistry, and mathematics, despite my chronic issues with the last of these subjects. The misguided rationale behind this choice was that success in mathematics would be an indicator of my mastery of science, and therefore carry more weight when I applied to university!

On the first day of high school, I had a change of heart, and asked Vice Headmaster Mr. G.G. Hall if I could substitute biology for mathematics, clearly a far more logical choice for a future physician. He replied that he would immediately check my score in "O" level biology. When he returned from his office, he informed me that I had achieved a score of 45 percent in this subject which, I knew, constituted a bare pass. While Americans might think 45 percent to be a shameful outcome, the scoring system in England was far more penal than across the pond.

Mr. Hall expressed his unhappiness about my request to switch to biology but, grudgingly, said that he would "give me a chance" to hold my own. I breathed an immense sigh of relief. He had clearly thrown down the gauntlet. On the spot, I decided that this was a challenge to be avidly pursued so that I could prove him wrong. And so I decided to commit the next two years of my life to this arduous task. Once you commit to skiing on the wrong slope, you usually need to keep going. And so it was to be.

A Solo Trip to the Continent

When I was 17, I embarked on my first independent overseas trip. My destination that summer was Cannes in the south of France, to be followed by some travelling around western Europe. Naturally, I was excited at the prospect of this new experience. I had enrolled in a four-week course at the

College International de Cannes. However, it quickly dawned on me that I could practice conversational French on the beach far more happily than in a stuffy classroom. Since I had arranged to meet up with a friend, Nigel Rodley, in Cannes, this idea sounded even better. The instructors at the college did not object to this request. Presumably, plenty of others before me had done likewise. Nigel, two or three years older than me, arrived in a red Mini Cooper. I was not yet driving and was very impressed by both the car and its very vivid color.

His mastery of French, as well as his obvious maturity, far exceeded mine. As we relaxed in the sun and checked out our surroundings, he quickly became acquainted with Chantalle, an attractive French girl who was to improve his mastery of the language even more. She always came to the beach with her friend Elizabeth. In order to gain Elizabeth's attention, I started to draw some meaningless shapes in the sand with one of my ever so handsome feet. This seemed a highly promising move for a novice flirter like me. Elizabeth, it turned out, was the niece of a well-recognized French composer of classical music, Albert Roussel. Delusions of a romance with a charming girl from such a noted background soon flooded my mind. Although this was not to be, we did become good friends for the duration of my stay.

Nigel's background greatly influenced his career. He lost many family members in the Holocaust. When his father escaped to England, he volunteered for the army and tragically died in 1944 during the landing at Arnhem. Nigel's mission in life then became an unrelenting fight for human rights. He was Amnesty International's first legal officer, visited 18 countries to improve conditions for political prisoners, and helped draft the United Nations convention against torture. For these and other services in support of global justice, he received a knighthood.

After enjoying the eye-opening beauty of Cannes and its surroundings, and saying goodbye to Nigel, I took the train to Geneva. There, fittingly, I saw the Palace of the League of Nations, where I imagine Nigel subsequently spent much time. From Geneva, I moved on to the majesty of the Swiss Alps, where I had the breathtaking experience of riding the Jungfraujoch railway to a height of more than 11,000 feet. I had, of course, never seen any sights remotely close to this, and kept shaking my head in disbelief. The next stops were Lugano in the Italian part of Switzerland, and Lake Como in northern Italy. In these areas, life was far more relaxed and peaceful. The trains slowed down, too. In Italy, they, or rather the Italians running them, adamantly refused to follow the timetable for which Swiss railways were renowned. It did not matter, since I happily idled time away amidst the beauty of the lakes and the surrounding countryside.

My Father Meets Donnie

It had been two or more years since my mother had died. Her loss had taken a huge toll on my father, even to the extent, as already mentioned, that he had contemplated suicide. It was quite a time before he regained his vigor, his humor, and a sense of purpose in life.

He then started to hold Sunday musical afternoons with delicious pastries as well as the inevitable sandwiches. I wondered if he was trying to re-live the mood of pre-war Austria, with its vibrant coffee houses and beautiful classical music. He was still fond of lieder, German art songs of the nineteenth century, and so my father played a lot of Schubert's lieder. He invited friends who were Jewish refugees from central Europe to these teas, knowing that such music would not be foreign to them. The women seemed less appreciative than their husbands and were more inclined to chatter while the men listened to these romantic, often plaintive melodies. This greatly irritated my father, and he would make this clear to all concerned by mouthing "psst," often repeating himself if he could not obtain the desired effect. He could also be quite rude to some of his guests. When one lady turned up in shiny black leather trousers, he loudly told her how terrible she looked in this garb. She had pretensions to a higher stratum of society and was quite offended by this remark. This, however, did not faze my father in the slightest.

About this time, my father started to go to sculpture classes, a form of artistic expression that he had previously explored. It was during these classes that he noticed a vivacious and charming younger lady whose name was Donnie Kendrick. They became friendly, and their relationship progressed until they were frequent companions. It was obvious to any observer that they were very much in love. In the eyes of the Jewish community, Donnie had several strikes against her: she was very young (in her twenties), very attractive, and, most culpably, was not Jewish. Because of this latter unforgivable sin, about half of my father's Jewish friends immediately stopped socializing with him. In situations like this, you quickly find out who are your real friends.

They had in mind for him a specific Jewish widow of somewhat better background, well educated, and in his age range. I knew her and could see that she was rather a cold fish. She was obviously not a match that suited my father who, behind his rather stern exterior, was a deeply sentimental person. His unwillingness to pursue her only added fuel to the fire exhibited by his soon-to-be ex-friends. While Donnie and I certainly had our differences, I was very glad that my father had found such happiness with her. Together, they took many trips to Europe, and Donnie quickly came to appreciate the different lifestyle in which she found herself. She even started, as a measure of her empathy, to start speaking with a European accent and became a relentless supporter of Israel and Zionism.

Donnie was very active as a volunteer at the Jewish residential home, Doniesthorpe Hall, in Leeds. She also took courses in alternative forms of healing, including Reiki therapy, which she employed to great effect on many friends and patients. Her vibrant, charming personality resulted in her becoming a featured guest on local radio for a considerable period of time. She was, all in all, a dynamic and very remarkable lady.

I did not understand how people in my father's world could be so cruel and unforgiving. Was it really so important to them that they needed to respond by cutting him out of their lives? Did they not care for his happiness and newfound love for life? This narrow mindedness had a profound effect on me, and subsequently came to affect the course that my future relationships would also take. I was now ambivalent about the society in which I had grown up, one that seemed both petty and provincial. Did we have to be so inward looking?

Reflections on Celibacy

Monks, whether Catholic, Buddhist, or practitioners of other faiths, characteristically remain single. This is, in large part, because celibacy is supposed to bring them closer to God and the service of the church. This may well be true. However, celibacy is not without its dangers. An estimated 300,000 children have been the victims of sexual abuse within the French Catholic church over the last 70 years, and such abuse occurs in many countries around the world. Shockingly, many of these men of God chose to do nothing about these crimes and even went to great lengths to hide them from the unsuspecting public. It is only in recent years that much of the nature and extent of these crimes have become known and appropriate action, finally, is beginning to take place.

The question clearly arises: was man meant to be celibate? The answer, though perhaps controversial is, I think, "no." Sexual activity, with or without marriage, is a widely accepted norm in our society. It seems both contradictory and hypocritical that an individual is expected to confess his or her sins to a priest who may well be guilty of child abuse. But presumably, this is likely not that uncommon.

When my father was 52, losing his wife left him utterly devastated. It was several years before he recovered from this enormous loss. Fortunately, celibacy was not in his blood and he very gradually resumed a life that was punctuated by relationships with other women. As already mentioned, my father and Donnie were clearly in love, and later married. She undoubtedly rescued my father and gave him a second life during which they spent many, very happy years together. Without Donnie, he would have been, I think, a lost soul. Celibacy was foreign to his nature, as it is to most men. The pressures of being celibate are, I think, a dangerous path to tread. The idealism of serving God, I believe, can wear remarkably thin if one concurrently shuns the opportunity of a partner in life. Man was intended to be in a relationship, not just with God, but also with a tangible human being.

High School and Application to Medical School

The teaching of science in high school was truly excellent, perhaps vindicating my parents' decision to transfer me to RGS. Physics remained a problem. Why, for example, do electrons move backwards? And why does it rain? I really did not care, as long as I carried an umbrella. I dreaded physics calculations and, since understanding the concepts of this subject were far beyond me, I memorized experiments by heart. Organic chemistry did have some appeal. It was taught by our form master, Mr. D.C. Hall, who explained its intricacies very clearly. Unlike physics, it involved logic. Zoology was engrossing, but the life and habits of plants did not exactly bowl me over. As my high school years progressed, I increasingly became a nerd fixated on mastering these rather alien subjects.

I took all this stuff very seriously. While pupils in my year were gallivanting around smoking, their school caps perched cheekily on the back of their heads as they hung out after hours with girls who they thought to be "forward," I remained solidly at my desk accumulating reams of information, mainly by rote and rarely by deduction. This paid off handsomely, however, and I was top of the class throughout my entire high school career. The challenge posed by Mr. G.G. Hall on that first day of high school had been more than met. I managed to score 65 percent in physics, 70 percent in chemistry and 75 percent (a distinction) in biology. These marks were rather more than the required 45 percent pass mark and boded well for my application to medical school. My delusions of attaining a much-vaunted state scholarship, however, were thwarted when I accidentally removed a rat's adrenal gland instead of merely pinning it. To make matters worse, I creatively interpreted a crack in the glass slide as a microorganism named Vaucheria attempting sexual reproduction, while completely missing a lone amoeba floating around elsewhere under the damned microscope.

A classmate, Roy Homburg, and I found out that no RGS student had ever attended a London medical school because their applications were never sufficiently early. Once we had cottoned on to this, we applied to all 12 (!) London medical schools in good time, many of which were prestigious but not necessarily better than those in the provinces which were quickly catching up.

Guy's Hospital was the most revered medical school in London, but it clearly was not prepared to review applications equitably, for its application form asked, "Did your father receive his medical training at Guy's?" Viennese shoemakers did not seem to fit in with this critical background check. Guy's Hospital also asked one's religion. Maybe they were searching for priests bent on becoming physicians, but that clearly was not my calling. Questions like these, steeped in tradition and racial prejudice, would not, of course, pass muster now.

Both of us hoped that Middlesex Hospital, being a more recent addition to the plethora of medical schools in London, would adopt a more democratic approach to selecting its student body. Roy was a highly accomplished athlete, and had been a mainstay of the high school teams at RGS in both rugby and cricket. I, the nerd, was a considerably better pupil, but was woefully short of sporting achievements. I clearly needed to "spin" this aspect of life to enhance my chances for admission. So, when asked about sporting achievements, I mentioned that I had played house (intramural) cricket without releasing the dates of this short-lived, prehistoric achievement. To bolster my case even further, I stated that I had been on the school tennis team. While I was named to the team on one occasion when our best players were all competing in more important events elsewhere, the match was rained out so I did not play. Still, my name was clearly printed on the team list. When all was said and done, Roy and I were delighted to find out that we had both been accepted to Middlesex Hospital Medical School. After our summer vacations, a new chapter of our lives was about to start!

Another Trip and A Broadening Worldview

My second European trip of independence, this time accompanied by Ashley Levi, took place in 1961 when I was 18. Our destination was a remote island named Ponza, about an hour by boat from Rome, where I had somehow discovered a student camp. After a long train journey, we arrived at Italy's glorious capital. There, we saw the iconic sights: St. Peters, the Forum Romanum and Coliseum, and the Spanish Steps, as well as other less well-known places of interest.

I also experienced my first live opera, "Turandot," not one of Verdi's better efforts, at the open-air Baths of Caracalla, which can accommodate, believe it or not, 20,000 people. If we had been there one night earlier, we would have seen "Aida" with live elephants parading in the opera's triumphal march. We had the cheapest seats in the amphitheater for, I think, 50 cents. This is, at least, what my carefully preserved ticket shows. Now, prices appear to be $50 to $250. Every attendee, including children, was smartly dressed. Italians take great pride in their appearance, unlike the lack of style so apparent throughout most of England.

Ponza is a volcanic island which, at that time, received very few foreign visitors. The student camp there was host to about 200 of us. Ashley and I stood out like sore thumbs, as virtually everyone else was Italian. We were befriended by a small group of older, highly likable Italians, to whom we must have seemed like fish out of water. Two Neapolitan brothers dominated this small group, and both were great fun and charming. Almost immediately, sensing our ignorance of Italian, they pressed us to introduce ourselves to others with a rather strong idiomatic question: "Quanta costa un buono pezzo de figa?" Let's say this roughly translates into, "What does a good piece of ass cost?" To avoid any risk of censorship, I will leave it at that. We had a wonderful time with these newly made friends. Perhaps they thought us bold by venturing into their midst. We swam in the warm water, sunbathed, and enjoyed both their company and the unspoiled beauty of the island. Finally, after a short boat trip to Naples, we returned to the mainland.

In Naples, the two brothers and their friends made us most welcome, while showing us their unbridled exuberance for life. They would ride their Vespa motorbikes at lunatic speeds down the cobbled, narrow streets of the city, but more impressive still was their social agenda. The brothers had a large bar, together with an improvised dance floor, in their home. With this in the background, serious partying including all manner of libations and much dancing took place starting, unbelievably, very early in the afternoon. These guys and gals clearly wasted no time with formalities. By this time, we were treated as one of them despite our obvious naïveté. It seemed to me that the Italians knew how to live! There was a fun-loving, passionate spontaneity about them that differed from the well-known English reserve.

Our final stop in Europe was Paris. As in Rome, we headed out to its landmark sights which included Notre Dame, the vast expanse of the Louvre and the Palace of Versailles. We paid special attention to our evening's entertainment. There were four nights open to us, and these were spent with visits to the exotic Folies Berger, the Opera Comique (which staged light opera), a theater showing the film "Exodus," and a rather nondescript strip club. In the latter location, we worked our way up to the front row, only to discover that the naked ladies were quite repulsive. Disappointed by this, we quietly let ourselves out from the back of the so-called theater. From there, we soon came to be relocated in the relative safety of our hometown Leeds.

After School, Stay Home or Play Away?

These two trips to Europe opened my eyes to other ways of living. It would have been easy to stay in Leeds, a provincial town in the north of England. I had a great set of friends there and had enjoyed many wonderful times with them. Leeds had a fine university, some lovely suburbs and even, at that time, a great soccer team. Yet I was strongly encouraged to leave by both my father and godfather. If I had stayed in these comfortable, protective surroundings, I would have had limited exposure to other cultures or people who behaved differently or looked differently to us. This constitutes a real trap, because we may then become afraid to venture out of our comfort zone.

As the world becomes increasingly globalized, I believe that we need to emerge from our childhood cocoons of safety and see what is out there. My main request to our children while they were still in high school was to apply to colleges far and wide, for, if they wished to stay attached to their background, it would still be there after college or whatever. There is a downside for parents, of course, for they may never return and staying connected would become harder. But we now have airplanes and FaceTime and much else, so all is not lost.

Leaving home is an adventure — an adventure, admittedly — that is not everyone's cup of tea. You need to establish new relationships and, often, you find yourself exploring new interests. But life is full of new avenues, dreams, and risks. I am clearly biased, though, since I have moved from town to town and country to country for most of my life. I have enjoyed the challenges, even if I found myself in unfamiliar and unsettling environments. Our two children benefited greatly from their moves to Philadelphia and Houston, and I think have very few regrets about leaving home and establishing their own, more independent lives. Don't most living beings have to learn to fend for themselves, instead of remaining in the comfortable bubble of their upbringing?

It is easy for me to pitch this line, but I do recognize that many offspring prefer to stay close to family and home and live in this protected environment. Some may fear the voyage into relatively uncharted territory and feel that the closeness of family and childhood friends is what matters most. If so, that is all well and good, as long as they keep their minds open to new ideas and show respect for their differences from other communities, cultures and religions. If we are unable to do this, I see little hope for progress in these heavily polarized times.

A Radical Change of Identity

In England, at the time, future physicians almost always started medical school at the age of 18. There was no need whatsoever to receive any undergraduate education at university. Before starting medical school in London, I received unequivocal advice from my father and godfather. They urged me to change my name before leaving home. This, they said, would level the playing field and save me from being exposed to both xenophobia and antisemitism. They were only too aware of Jewish neighbors of ours who had a brilliant son. He had been denied medical posts because his name was Salinsky, a name both foreign and Jewish. And so I was persuaded to make a momentous decision that would change my whole life. The weekend before starting medical school, I changed my name by deed poll from "Kohut" to "Kelvin." No longer would the name Kohut be mutilated into "Cowhut" or other similarly undignified variants.

This change of name provided the perfect opportunity to avoid any semblance of Jewishness. It facilitated a complete change of identity, a change that had been gradually gathering steam since those times long ago when I had ceased to practice any religious ritual. The intolerance of my father's Jewish friends to Donnie, and my expanded world view after seeing chunks of European life and culture over the past two years, played a big part in this metamorphosis.

Clearly, this was a huge turning point in my life. I was not just becoming an independent teenager, for I had now assumed a radically different identity as I was about to enter medical school. Was life merely a stage on which you chose different roles as time went by? While I was glad to leave provincialism behind, was I ready to both pursue my career in a different, more sophisticated location but also, more uncertainly, in the guise of being a different person? While this made me a little nervous, it was also undeniably exciting. It did, however, in no way make me understand who the hell I was or where I belonged. I was about to become, unwittingly or otherwise, an urban nomad. It was the beginning of an interesting voyage to many different ports, without the close presence of either my father or of dear friends. I had little idea of what lay ahead.

PART THREE

EARLY ADULTHOOD: LONDON AND MORE

Looking Back on my New World

As a young adult I found myself thrust into an entirely new world, not just professionally but also socially and culturally. When I look back now, I am aware of the many ways that I was tossed around between my different identities in different communities and how the flow of this new life carried me far away from my roots.

I am now struck by the way my career goals, with their attached required examinations, pushed me inexorably forward. Even when those goals were not immediately clear, I was so busy moving forward, striving to hit one target after another, that there was not much time for reflection.

I regret none of this. It is part of being young and living one's life. But it is interesting to look back on this time and realize how disturbing it must have been to go from one exam to another exam to yet another exam at the same time as trying to find my feet in these new worlds. And then to land in the United States of all places at the end of it!

The anecdotes I share now reflect some of that sense of ambition and determination that drove me forward, and the many different social and travel experiences in which I became engaged.

The North/South Divide

Five Jewish boys, including me, started university or medical school in one or another of London's many colleges. All of us stayed in a very pleasant dormitory run by a kind lady named Mrs. Gill. Sharing this dormitory with the others made life very affordable. Furthermore, the house was in a lovely part of London across the road from Regent's Park, and I was within walking distance of the medical school. The five of us rarely socialized together since, apart from Roy Homburg and myself, we were attending different institutions. With my newfound name, people that I came across in my first two years or so in London were completely unaware that I was Jewish. Undoubtedly, a certain guilt associated with this blatant deception troubled me, consciously and subconsciously, for many years.

The makeup of my medical school class clearly illustrated the north/south divide that existed, and still exists, in England. Half the class hailed, like me, from the gritty, industrialized north of England. We were not considered the equal of the other half of our class, most of whom came from the gentler southern parts of the country and had often attended boarding schools. Southerners were wealthier, more reserved, and had access to better education as well as, in those days, more culture. All of these factors served to underscore England's longstanding divisive, class-conscious society. Northerners and southerners were like oil and water, clearly immiscible. It was as if there were two separate and distinct countries, each wary of the other. Many northerners headed south for greener pastures but moves by southerners in the opposite direction were frowned upon and rare.

Fiona Hill, a Russia expert who served under three presidents, and who gave important testimony at the Trump impeachment trial, emphasizes the north/south divide very clearly. Throughout most of her illustrious career, including that at Harvard, she was repeatedly asked three questions: Where do you come from? What does your father do? What school did you go to? Her answers were, respectively, Bishop Auckland, coal mining and a comprehensive school. Her harsh upbringing in the industrialized wastelands of the northeast, and her father's lowly regarded job, as well as her failure to attend a grammar school, all branded her as a professionally unacceptable individual, irrespective of her brilliant accomplishments. Even at Harvard, she was not considered the equal of other students. Being a woman was yet another stab in the back.

In England, one's accent immediately indicates your background to the listener. Although there are varieties of northern accent, they are all very different from the softer "plum in your mouth" accent of the well-bred southerner. As I stayed in the south throughout my training, my northern (Yorkshire) accent gradually came to sound plummier and plummier and, when I returned home for visits, the Yorkshire accent came ever more sharply into focus.

The big question looming for me, of course, was whether I would succeed in "changing sides." Migrating to London with a new, anglicized name clearly suggested that this was my game plan. If I was looking for Jewish students in my class, there were only two, apart from Roy and me, and it seemed to me that both of them had also relinquished their Jewishness. They were, however, from the south and we never came close to discussing our respective backgrounds.

Pre-Clinical Studies Or "When You Keep Your Hands off Living Patients"

The first year and a half of medical school was classified as pre-clinical. It was entirely devoted to anatomy, physiology, histology, and pharmacology. For much of our time in anatomy, under the erudite leadership of Professor Walls, we dissected an unhappy corpse from head to toe. When I say "we," this pointless exercise was essentially carried out by four guys wielding knives with great dexterity. Any clumsy intrusion of mine could, and would, have negated all their careful hard work. I did, however, trim the toenails of our corpse in an effort to make him more socially acceptable.

I found physiology far more interesting. It was taught by Professor Neil, who had a wry sense of humor. During one of his lectures, he asked our Lebanese classmate how such-and-such a condition was treated back in his country. Without batting an eyelid, the student replied: "We cut off one of their ears." None of us approached him afterwards to inquire whether this was indeed true. Histology was taught by Professor Gould, who gave this inconsequential subject some much-needed relevance. In his class, I remember learning much about mitochondria, knowing full well that I would never see one ever again. Pharmacology was absorbing, and I realized that it lay the groundwork for an understanding of the medications that, one day, we would all be prescribing.

There were three students from abroad in our class of 54 students. One, Wole, was from Nigeria and he easily assimilated with the rest of us. Another, Wilfred, was from neighboring Ghana, and it was quickly obvious that mingling with us was extremely uncomfortable for him. We tried to make him feel welcome, but it was to no avail. The third foreign student was the classmate from Lebanon. He spent much of his time playing cards in nearby Soho, had an unusually long fifth fingernail, and was widely considered to be a cardsharp. One lunch break, he was playing poker with three others in our class. One of them accused him of cheating, whereupon he pulled out a knife and threatened to use it. Fortunately, he was overcome (the other three were solidly built rugby players), and so he was unable to lop off any of their ears. All three of the foreign classmates, we found out, were privileged citizens of their respective countries to which they would each return and, at a national level, would then be placed in charge of whatever medical subspecialty they had chosen.

Half of our class, as already mentioned, were from the southern parts of England whereas the rest of us were from the provinces far north of London. While we were treated with civility by our more sophisticated classmates, we were never made to feel entirely at home on our newfound turf. It turned out that there was no difference in the level of academic performance between the two halves of the class, despite the exalted pedigree of those from the south. In our later clinical years, we were joined by students from Oxford and Cambridge because of insufficient patients in their teaching hospitals. While there were a few brilliant transplants from Oxbridge, there were many others who seemed complacent and very satisfied with their lot in life. I had expected them to be far sharper.

Professor Walls was born and trained in Glasgow. He was a distinguished, almost cadaveric gentleman well suited to anatomy. And well suited he was, for with his impeccable dress code he cut a striking figure from the moment he entered the lecture theater. He taught anatomy with meticulous attention to detail, and his lectures were always lucidly and beautifully delivered. At some point during one of his orations, he stopped and, looking directly at me, asked: "And whereaboots in Scotland do ye come from?" This was a showstopper because, with this one question, he had effectively blown my cover. There was no answer that I could meaningfully give, so, for once, I stayed silent. Maybe there was no malicious intent, but it felt like a blow well below the belt and an invisible shudder ran through my entire body.

Looking into the derivation of my name later that day, I discovered that "Kelvin" was essentially a Scottish name, referring to a river in Glasgow that flowed near our professor's beloved university. William Thompson, the famed physicist and mathematician from Glasgow, took the title "Lord Kelvin" in honor of the river, and the Kelvin temperature scale was later named after him. Clearly, my unwitting choice of name was an unmistakable error for those in the "know."

A Visit with my Yugoslavian Family

At the end of my first year of medical school, in 1962, I travelled with a group of my childhood friends by train across Europe to Split, a large town on the Yugoslavian coast. From there, we were passengers on a freight ship that took us further south, to Dubrovnik. Being impecunious, we all slept on deck. Dubrovnik was a strong maritime threat to Venice in the 14th and 15th centuries. With the breakup of Yugoslavia in the early 1990s, it was subject to siege by Serbia and much of the historic old part of the city was destroyed. However, its protective wall survived. After the war, the old city inside the walls was meticulously restored to its former appearance. The walk on this famed wall provided stunning views of the Adriatic Sea on one side, and views of the old city with its cobbled streets and red-roofed buildings on the other.

From Dubrovnik, I travelled alone to Belgrade to stay with my great uncle Benno and his family. His two children, Bogdan and Olga, also lived in Belgrade, together with their spouses. While there, I went to a clinic where Olga's husband, Mile, was seeing patients. There were quite a number of healthy-looking young males with large carbuncles on their necks or arms. I asked Mile how this could happen. He said that, when these youths were drunk, they would stick each other with the sharp ends of broken bottles. In this part of the world, it was clear that passions ran high.

Bogdan's wife Nada surprised me with detailed information and photographs of the concentration camps established by the Ustase in 1941, in the name of the Independent State of Croatia, a puppet state of Fascist Italy and Nazi Germany. The largest of these notorious camps was, as I have mentioned, Jasenovac. In all, several hundred thousand prisoners were cruelly slaughtered there, the exact number of which remains the subject of much dispute.

Bogdan then drove me 400 miles at an alarmingly rapid speed to Rovinj on the Istrian peninsula, where my Serbian relatives had a small, relatively primitive summer home. When water was needed, it was drawn up from a well on their property. In Rovinj, I rejoined my Leeds friends. Rovinj had a charming Italianate feel and, indeed, was only 60 miles from Trieste. We enjoyed its old town, its harbor, and nearby beaches. I loved meeting up again with Benno and his daughter Olga, both of whom had very happily stayed with us in Leeds but, as they aged, the connection sadly diminished.

Churchill and Nureyev: Brushes with Fame

The year 1962 brought an important patient to the hospital of our medical school. Winston Churchill, who was 87 years old at the time, had fallen over in his room at the Hotel de Paris in Monte Carlo. In doing so, he fractured the neck of his left femur. He was immediately flown home ("Remember, I want to die in England," he famously said), whereupon he was admitted to the Woolavington Wing at Middlesex Hospital. This wing was exclusively for private patients. Its building was made possible by the generosity of Baron Woolavington, a whisky baron who apparently paid, at least in part, for this honor.

There, Sir Winston was operated upon by two well-known orthopedic surgeons, Mr. Phillip Newman and Professor Herbert Seddon. One nurse was assigned to look after him, and no one else, during his hospital stay. Understandably, she found this somewhat nerve-racking. It is unclear whether he was allowed his much-favored drink, whisky, during his recovery and, if so, whether it came from one of the baron's distilleries. However, after a post-operative course that was complicated by a deep vein thrombosis, all was well and he was discharged home where, undoubtedly, his whisky was waiting for him.

I had an interesting experience with one girlfriend. She was a law student but had managed to get a part-time gig as chief undresser to the leading ballerina in a Sadlers Wells production. I asked if she could get me a similar gig for a male dancer and so was assigned one evening to a third or fourth ranking dancer. At the intermission, when he came to the dressing room, he was bleeding quite heavily from an untoward fall on the stage. He was appropriately bandaged and managed to carry on. After the intermission, I was allowed into the wings to see how the performance was progressing. To my utter amazement, about 10 yards from me was Rudolph Nureyev pacing angrily to and fro. I felt it best to keep my distance from him for he looked none too happy. I found out later that evening that he had choreographed the piece being performed, and he was very upset at how the dancers were mauling his choreography. It is not often that one has the chance to see a legend close up, angry or otherwise.

For Every Arduous Exam Course, There's a Pub

The pre-clinical period of one and a half years was punctuated by an examination towards its end that determined whether you could progress to the forthcoming three clinical years. If you failed, you remained in limbo for another six months. One third of the class fell into the latter category, because there were insufficient hospital beds to accommodate us all, especially with the influx of a considerable number of Oxbridge students. I still had a high "nerd index" and spent many hours in the library. This enabled me to be in the top ten percent or so of the class and I thereby passed this examination rather painlessly.

Across the road from the medical school was a pub, the Rose and Crown. Prior to coming to London, I think that I had only once entered a pub. It was, at that time, not considered part of the Jewish way of life. The father of one of my close friends in Leeds, a delightful and highly educated fellow, would go for a weekly drink to a nearby local pub. For this unacceptable transgression, he was widely considered to be an alcoholic. The legal drinking age in England was 18. Some of us first-year medical students were under this age, but the owners of the pub, The Rose and Crown, never questioned any of us about this.

Throughout medical school, but especially in the clinical years, about one third of the class would spend most evenings in The Rose and Crown. The medical students that made the pub their second home had finetuned their approach to examinations. They would stop their nightly boozing and pick up the books with just sufficient time to pass these end-of-term tests. I assume students in the years above had advised them at what point they needed to move from the pub to the library. Most of them, it should be said, later appeared to become doctors capable of sound judgement. Could the camaraderie and drinking, I wondered, have helped them mature?

English Doctors in Training Don't Know What They're Doing: It's the System

Most of us were rather nervous about starting our first clinical year. At our sister hospital, the Central Middlesex Hospital, we were expected to be in the frontline for evaluating emergency room patients. I carried a stiff five-by seven-inch card in my pocket which contained the names and doses of the twelve or so most frequently used drugs for treating these acutely ill patients. It was often potluck as to what choice I would make. If the patient failed to respond to my pick, then and only then were we allowed to discuss the situation with our resident. You may wonder what a 20-year-old was doing making such important decisions, but training in England was very much on the "sink or swim" principle, quite different from the closely supervised approach in the United States.

Especially in the main teaching hospital, the Middlesex Hospital, our clinical teachers were, for the most part, very aloof and forbidding characters. One never spoke or asked them a question unless they first spoke to you. We always addressed the consultants as "Sir" and, as there were several who had already been knighted by the Queen, for them this form of address was highly appropriate. We would always gather in the main lobby of the hospital entrance to greet them upon their ceremonious arrival. Most of their time, of course, was spent accumulating wealth in their private rooms in and around Harley Street where they saw patients of considerable means.

We were divided into groups, or firms, of five who would go on clinical rounds with our consultant for that month. Our group was clearly not in the top echelon. Two of the firm were Welshmen who were perennial pub-crawlers. While they were great guys, they could not be relied upon to field questions asked by the consultant. A third member of our firm was Bosko, who hailed from Sibenik in Croatia. He was very amiable, but even less informed about our patients' diseases than the Welshmen, if that was indeed possible. It was left to Bernie, a well-read guy from South Africa, and I, to hold the fort. Naturally Bernie and I became good friends, for we needed a joint strategy for our firm to stay on its feet. This was, at times, stressful as the other three clearly were not that interested in making any useful contributions beyond the confines of the pub.

Early during our first medical rotation, we had to complete a thorough history and examination of a patient, write it up and then present the findings to our consultant. The three slackers on my firm decided to play a game with me. They arranged for my first patient to be a highly attractive and heavily made up young woman who could well have passed for, and may well have been, a call girl. My physical examination required that I perform both a rectal and vaginal examination. I was uneasy about handling this situation, and I am sure the patient could sense my apprehension. Nevertheless, we both survived this tense ordeal.

Each morning, we were expected to draw blood from our patients for one or more tests, such as white cell counts, electrolytes, or whatever. My dexterity was, as usual, very limited. It took me twice as long as the others to withdraw the requisite amount of blood. We used rather long metal needles in those days. On one occasion, I thought I had entered the vein, then advanced the needle, only to be horrified to see the needle emerge through the skin at a site well beyond the vein. I blinked in disbelief. Fortunately, the patient was quite unaware of this misadventure.

Young and Rootless in London

During these early years in London, I changed my accommodation on several occasions. After Mrs. Gill's, Ashley Levi (now Lawrence, constituting another Jewish lad who succumbed to name-changing) and I went to live in a small apartment off Baker Street, close to the fictitious Sherlock Holmes House at 221B Baker Street. Our kitchen was part of a long room with the toilet at the other end. I am sure this was illegal, but the price was right and so we stayed there for a while. Later, I moved into slightly more hygienic digs in Putney, where I shared an apartment with Bob Elkeles, a very bright guy in the year above me. Bob was secretary of the medical school tennis team, and persuaded me to play second doubles, the lowest position, on that team. I do not believe we ever came even remotely close to winning a match. The tennis was played on grass, which was great fun. Later, Ashley asked me to join him in a very expensive apartment in Montague Mansions, again very near Baker Street. He was avidly pursuing an elegant, well-brought-up Jewish girl, Yvonne, who lived with her parents in the neighboring building. I assume this close proximity gave him an advantage over more distant suitors. He devoted a lot of time and a great deal of money to this pursuit. I concluded that my main role was to help him pay the rent, for we rarely socialized together. His dedicated attention to Yvonne paid off, for he eventually married her.

Opportunities to meet nurses now presented themselves. The medical students organized frequent "hops," at which quite a number of nurses from our adjacent nursing school would come over and join us to drink (not excessively) and dance (not too loosely). Other than for a very carefully monitored entrance, their residence across the street was always strictly off limits. My dancing efforts still fell considerably short of Fred Astaire's. Despite this continuing handicap, I met two or three girls who I subsequently dated. All were non-Jewish. Actually, I do not remember seeing any Jewish nurses among them, for this was not their prime territory.

I also went to an extraordinary number of plays in the West End, which I thoroughly enjoyed, usually from the very cheapest seats in the house. Occasionally, I would even find a way to quietly crash a rehearsal, which was exciting. I started to go to opera performances, at times even managing to see productions at the Royal Opera House in Covent Garden. Opera fascinated me, with its great drama, beautiful voices, and sumptuous scenery and costumes. Later in my training, I discovered that, if I ran fast enough from the relatively inexpensive English National Opera to the nearby Royal Opera House, the doorman there would let me sit in the balcony for the last act at no charge. That way,

I witnessed the dramatic entombment scene of Radames, the Egyptian general, and Aida, the Ethiopian princess. It left a lasting impression on my vacuous mind.

I sometimes visited a gentle, delightful distant cousin of my father's, Hilde Farago, who lived in Wembley Park. At times her equally charming son, John, would join us (much more about John later!). Occasionally I played golf, but this required a ride on the Underground of at least 45 minutes that clearly limited the frequency with which I could play. My golf partner was a guy in the year above me, Chris Royston. This association was later to prove quite useful. I made no attempt whatsoever to connect with the Jewish community that was based north of Central London. Its unofficial headquarters was Golders Green, sometimes affectionately referred to as "Goldberg Green." Although my social life was somewhat in limbo, I had no yearning to reconnect with my Jewish counterparts for I was pursuing an entirely different role.

First Trip to Israel

For a month during our clinical years, we could elect to study at a hospital abroad. The term "study" was clearly an exaggerated one, for the commitment was not at all arduous. For this elective, as I had never been to Israel, I chose to spend the month at the Hadassah Medical Center in Jerusalem. Approaching the port of Haifa in Israel was quite an emotional experience and made me think of the ship "Exodus" which, in 1947, was carrying many Holocaust survivors to Palestine. When close to the harbor, the British intervened and the hapless passengers were returned to Europe where most were compelled to go to displacement camps. Viva good old Britannia, the land of hope and glory!

Once in Jerusalem, I was amazed to find the Hadassah Medical Center to be far better equipped than my teaching hospital in London. We were a large body of students hailing from many different countries and were treated to fascinating lectures as well as given the opportunity to visit the great religious sites of the city. Even better, we were allowed to take off for long, three-day weekends and explore different parts of the country.

I did so with several newly made friends. I was particularly friendly with a male Austrian student, whose name escapes me, and a female Irish student, Carla, whose name does not. A favorite destination was Akhziv on Israel's northern coast. It was there that a well-known eccentric, Eli Avivi, had founded the self-proclaimed state of Akhzivland on a small, but beautiful, hippie slice of coastline. After some regulatory issues, the Israeli government had finally allowed Eli's innocent nonsense to prevail. There is now even a signpost to point drivers in the right direction. Of course, no passport or visa is needed to enter this whimsical, make-believe state.

While in Israel, I took the opportunity to spend time with my paternal uncle, Hans, and his family. Hans was an extraordinary railway buff, knowing literally everyone working on the Israeli trains (there were not that many), and was very familiar with the details of most of the world's railway systems. He had two children and several grandchildren. The family dynamic between his two children was, unfortunately, extremely hostile. His son Abi was, like my father, an outstanding swimmer. Standing next to his tall, muscular torso, my skinny body made me look many years younger than him. This was my first visit to Israel and, despite the tension, I enjoyed meeting this branch of my father's family. I found Israelis to be very direct and face-to-face, which was refreshing. They were easy to converse with and, despite their bluntness, were extremely warm and friendly.

Finding My Way in Medicine and Avoiding Insanity

When I entered medical school, it was, as I mentioned, with the intention of becoming a psychiatrist. So, when the psychiatry rotation started, I studied even more diligently than usual, and won the class prize in this subject. However, during the rotation, I concluded that virtually all my teachers had issues, whether mental or psychosomatic or both. One, for example, had an uncontrollable facial twitch, and most of the others exhibited weird personality traits. I was well aware that some physicians chose psychiatry, at least in part, to sort themselves out. Since I had diagnosed myself as having nothing more than mild chronic anxiety during this rotation, I saw no reason to choose psychiatry as a career on this basis.

Most inpatient psychiatry involved looking after bipolar or schizophrenic patients which made me think that, even if you started out relatively normal, you might eventually develop some form of mental disorder! There is an old joke: "If, when talking to a patient, you feel you are going crazy, then that person is likely a schizophrenic." Who needs that kind of experience? It came as a surprise to me that I was now abandoning my goal of becoming a psychiatrist. Although I certainly talk more than most (!), I am capable of being a good listener and it has always interested me why people take the actions that they do rather what these actions are. The question "why" is frequently hard to figure out and so, it seems, is often avoided. Perhaps that was part of the attraction of psychiatry.

Having discarded the notion of becoming a psychiatrist, I now had to consider a different choice of specialty. So, what other fields of medicine came to mind? Surgery was out of the question, for I could barely tie a knot. Manual dexterity, or rather complete lack thereof, precluded this specialty or any variant of it. Being confronted by any contraption that needed fingering to make it function was unquestionably quite beyond me. And so I concluded, mainly by a process of exclusion, that I might become an internist, and I now made this my intended goal.

I later did a one-week locum tenens (a temporary internship) at my teaching hospital, thinking it might enhance my chances of getting a full internship there. The locum position gave you the opportunity to function as an intern ahead of time, so that you could see how you measured up. As a student, you have only a superficial view of how patients are managed, whereas as an intern you see just how much hard work this entails. My consultant for this week-long trial was a short, intense endocrinologist, Dr. J.D.N. Nabarro. Every day, he ordered all kinds of stimulation and suppression tests of the endocrine glands. I had to place these orders and keep track of the results, at a pace that was far too fast for my addled mind. To add fuel to the fire, many of these tests were quite complex. I was in over my head and knew it.

My medical school training was completed successfully in June 1966. Becoming qualified as a doctor at 23 years of age had always struck me as insane, but such was the nature of the beast. It was now time to see if I could get that much-vaunted internship at my teaching hospital. There were only 12 or so places available for our class of 54 students. Despite being in the top 10 to 15 percent of my class, I was not offered one of these spots. Perhaps my slippery performance in Dr. Nabarro's domain had not helped, or maybe my superiors sensed that my practical skills were not of the highest order.

My First Internship: An Eye-Opening Experience

Faced with finding my first internship, my golfing buddy Chris Royston came to my rescue. Chris set up an interview for me with Mr. Max Pemberton. In England, I should explain, fully trained male surgeons assume the title of "Mr."

instead of "Dr." This can be traced back to earlier times when surgeons were "barber surgeons," and did not need to go to university.

At the appointed time, I met Mr. Pemberton, a tall, ruddy-faced man who immediately offered me a glass of sherry. I took this to be a good omen. He asked me about my performance in medical school, and I told him that I was in the top ten or fifteen percent of the class. There were no further questions about my medical training. Chris had primed me about his forthcoming questions, and of their paramount importance. "Do you play much tennis?" he asked. That one was easy, for I loved the game. Next, he inquired about my experience with squash. This was a little trickier. I said, truthfully, that I had played only a few times, hastily adding that I hoped to improve my abilities in that more rarefied sphere of activity. Finally, came the stinger: "Did I sail?" I did not, but I told him of my willingness to learn and how I would love to have the opportunity. That sealed the deal, and I became house surgeon to Mr. Max Pemberton at Chase Farm Hospital on the outskirts of London. There was now no need to scout around in the uncouth north of the country, to my great relief!

During this internship, I was to play many games of tennis, a few games of squash, and sail occasionally with my surgical boss. For my first experience sailing with him, I accompanied him, his wife, and a hamper of food to a comfortable spot on the Thames estuary. There, he told her that he would first take me for a sail on the river, and then drop me off so she could then replace me. Off we went, and we travelled quite a distance. I was sufficiently nervous that I went into acute retention and, only with difficulty, was able to relax enough to empty my bladder overboard. We turned around, and, as we approached the spot where his wife was sitting, he showed no signs of going ashore and just kept on sailing. Based on this, and many later episodes, it was quite clear that he needed an intern as a recreational diversion from his wife. Any surgical assistance that I could offer was decidedly of much less importance.

And I was truly of little surgical assistance. One time, I fell asleep while holding the retractor to keep the liver at bay. This shortcoming was not at all welcome, as it resulted in this large organ protruding well into my boss's operative field. After a loud "wakey wakey" from him, I came around and regained control of the liver with my large metallic instrument.

One of my other duties was to perform, unaided, a list of minor operative procedures. I looked forward to these experiences about as much as I wished to visit hell. There was one poor chap who had several sebaceous cysts on his head. Each one, of course, required local anesthesia before I wielded my clumsy blade. Once I plunged into his scalp with my instruments of torture, each area became flooded with rivers of blood. Further details are rather gory and do not merit discussion. However, no one fainted. After some time, I completed these onerous excisions, and both the patient and I lived to fight another day. Most surgical interns were given the opportunity to remove an inflamed appendix. It was considered a badge of honor. I was neither given nor wanted this chance, for it would have terrified me.

In the hospital, my eyes were opened to a lot of behavior by the medical staff that I can only describe as distinctly amoral, the likes of which I could hardly believe. I was told, on good authority, that surgical residents frequently jumped on top of a nurse lying on the operating table when the surgical list was finally completed. I will leave it to your imagination to guess which muscles would indeed then be flexed. At least once, a Greek anesthesiologist came by the nurses' desk on my ward and suggested, using a very crude metaphor, that they take advantage of the opportunity to engage in oral sex with him. And these guys were doctors! My upbringing in Leeds had not prepared me for any of this, and so it took me quite a while to process it all.

Skiing for the First Time

That winter, I went skiing for the first time. I chose to go to Livigno in Italy, previously a haven for smuggling but now a respectable ski resort. Arriving there without any skills seemed rather daunting, so I went to the Lillywhite's sports store in Piccadilly Circus which had a short, dry ski slope. As well as being short, it was also not steep. As a result, coming to a stop was both effortless and automatic. Emboldened by this advanced level of training, I arrived in Livigno. In ski school the next day, I found myself one class above the beginner level, because I had already "skied." It took me a while, though, to learn how to fall. For me, reaching the ground was only accomplished by a mixture of awkward twists and turns of the torso. After mastering this basic problem, I was able to graduate from the bunny slopes to the easier of the intermediate blue runs. We were taught the now old-fashioned stem christie turn, which was safe but slow. For those runs that were relatively straight, turns were clearly unnecessary.

The very exalted Ski Club of Great Britain had a group there and they sometimes allowed me to ski with them, albeit at my slower pace. On the last day, the club organized a race. I checked out the terrain well ahead of time and realized that turning was barely required. As a result, I did quite well. The organizers were impressed and invited me to ski with them in the afternoon. It was then that I recognized the need for technical proficiency. I really had not made much progress at all.

Towards the end of this exciting week in Livigno, I met a physiotherapist who was training in London named Wendy Davison, who said that, on our return, she would invite me to her next party. What was there to lose? I happily accepted this offer and, fortuitously, we exchanged contact information.

The Gloom of Radiotherapy, Jacqui, and the Possibility of Radiology

Arriving back in London, I started my second internship, this time at my teaching hospital. This internship was in radiotherapy. I believe that I secured this position after an animated conversation with one of the radiotherapy consultants over the net at a recent staff/student tennis match. In retrospect, it seemed that my two internships had been acquired on the basis of who I knew rather than what I knew. I was starting to learn how much this mattered.

When Wendy's party eventually materialized, I met a young woman wearing an exotic cheongsam who caught my eye from the other end of the room. A cheongsam is a figure-flattering, east Asian long dress. She did not seem to be with anyone and so, playing my strong (and only) card, I engaged her in my usual irreverent brand of conversation. I took great care to withhold any attempt at dancing until the ice was firmly broken.

Her name was Jacqui. She was a physiotherapist at my teaching hospital who was vivacious, attractive, and had that oh-so-much vaunted southern accent characteristic of London and its surrounds. With her, I would escape from the gloom and doom of the wards that I was assigned to cover. She had a bevy of friends, also physiotherapists, with whom she lived in nearby Swiss Cottage. They, too, were great fun. Almost immediately, Jacqui and I started dating.

Working on the radiotherapy wards, of which there were four, was very depressing. In those days, malignancies that led to hospitalization were almost always incurable. None of the patients knew their real diagnosis and, therefore, their likely outcomes. This was very stressful for the nurses, as they were always dodging the patients' questions. On one occasion, one patient found out that some of her "bad cells" had not been removed during surgery, and she started to spread the word. The nurses were in panic mode as they feared that soon the whole ward would know that they too might have a malignant tumor. I brought this matter up with the psychiatrist who was offering support to these unfortunate patients. His response was that, by telling them the truth, any glimmer of hope would be shattered, and the patients would then have nothing to hold onto. How things have changed since then!

Once a week, we went to the radiology department to look at our patients' X-rays with the radiologist, Dr. Brian Kendall. I was fascinated by what the X-rays revealed, and always looked forward to these visits. Since I had thrown psychiatry under the bus and was now considering internal medicine for my future career, it occured to me that I had a potential alternative, radiology. I made inquiries about what it took to find a residency in this subspecialty. While not essential, if you were seeking a radiology post anywhere in the south of the country, you first needed to be "boarded" in internal medicine.

Clearly then, whether I sought internal medicine or radiology as a career, it was going to be necessary to pass the internal medicine boards, the notorious M.R.C.P. (Member of the Royal College of Physicians) examination. This was the equivalent of the American boards in internal medicine, but far harder. The pass rate for the M.R.C.P. was about 30 percent, and many candidates, even good ones, took this examination two or more times before succeeding. Following this, toward the end of your training in radiology, you took your second board examinations, but this time in radiology, which was a far easier proposition. Nevertheless, a career in radiology in a favored part of the country appeared to require a long and arduous period of training.

Growing Closer to Jacqui and Further from My Roots

During the summer of 1967, Jacqui and I, together with our best friends Janet and her boyfriend Chris, took off for travels through France, and then on to Venice. On the way down, I remember Chris telling me that I needed to put my foot down more with Jacqui, rather than letting her make most of the calls. It was easy for him to give advice, but hard for me to implement his suggestions! Jacqui was very strong willed, and I considerably less so. As I look back, but did not realize at the time, my determination in pursuing my career led me to pay insufficient attention to outside relationships. My natural tendency has always been to take a more carefree approach to life beyond that of work. Of course, it is so very easy to indulge in Hindsight 101!

Venice was very special. With no roads, transport was either on foot or by water bus. This meant it was very quiet. Also, it was small enough that you could explore its streets and canals without needing to look more than occasionally at a map. The Grand Canal was indeed grand, and St. Mark's Square, even though filled with tourists, was strikingly impressive. We spent some time in the Swiss Alps on the way back. Throwing snowballs in the summer was a new experience.

Over the next year or so, we made other trips in our home country, including to the north where Jacqui met my father and Donnie, and to the Lake District where I had spent many happy childhood holidays. We also spent time with Jacqui's parents, who lived in Lindfield, a charming small village south of London. I was particularly fond of her mother, who was a very warm and gracious lady. Clearly, the acorn had not fallen very far from the tree.

It was beginning to look like I had entirely deserted my Jewish roots and was in the process of morphing into an essentially non-Jewish southerner. When we went back to Leeds, this change in my attitude came into sharper focus. Despite the very different upbringings of Jacqui and myself, the waters were not too choppy, and my father liked Jacqui. It was good to see that my father and Donnie remained very happy in each other's company and to know that they were enjoying many very pleasurable holidays together.

Yet Another Internship, and those Boards

In July 1967, I started another internship in medicine in Bedford, which was only 45 minutes away from London. This internship was not very exciting, but was useful for gaining further clinical experience as well as some much-needed time to study for part one of the dreaded M.R.C.P. One aspect of my time there had a huge impact on me. I accompanied one of my consultants, Dr. Bayliss, to see some private patients after he had completed his day's National Health Service obligations. Private practice greatly increased a physician's earnings. In one half day of seeing private patients, you could double (yes, double!) what you had earned in the socialized National Health Service during the remainder of the week.

The sight of a truly skilled and compassionate physician still seeing patients at eight, or even nine, o'clock, led me to conclude that internal medicine was not for me. My heart was now moving far more towards radiology, which, at that time, was basically a 9:00 a.m. to 5:00 p.m. job. I realized that I had no desire to spend endless hours asking patients a stream of questions late into the evening, questions that they frequently answered in an oblique and very unhelpful way and therefore had to be repeated. That was not how I wanted to spend the rest of my working life. I cared about patients and their treatment, but there were time limits to my compassion!

Furthermore, I was rather inept at the practical side of patient care. My physical examinations were probably no better than average, and when it came to any kind of procedure, I was often a potential danger to the well-being of the patient. I was originally drawn to the field of psychiatry because it seemed a challenge to understand how a patient thought, a challenge that was not dependent on checking up on the patient's body. I always enjoyed studying but was far less capable at the bedside. Radiology, I concluded, was far better suited to my more theoretical mindset than internal medicine.

Be More Jewish

I was best man for Bernard Olsburgh's wedding in December 1967. It was a lovely occasion and his bride, Susan, was delightful. Interestingly, despite being Jewish, she had been educated in a convent school where she rose to be head girl. How was that possible, I wondered? Catholics and Jews historically had never been the warmest of bedfellows. A guest at the wedding had a major heart attack, and Bernard (and I) administered cardiopulmonary resuscitation. I suspect that this was performed, in the main, by Bernard, with me watching at a carefully measured distance from the scene.

At this Jewish wedding, I was taken to one side by Bernard's mother, and forced to listen to her admonition and advice. She said it was all very well to "practice" on non-Jewish girls, but very important that I marry someone of the Jewish faith. By this time, I had been dating Jacqui for almost a year. The advice, though well-intentioned, fell on deaf ears. I received the same advice at the wedding of another of my Jewish friends. While I understood their point, I refused to let it impact my situation. I had broken with my Jewish heritage and had no interest in falling back into the comfortable social nest that it had provided. I was, on the other hand, very keen to keep pushing myself into the still somewhat unfamiliar world of non-Jewish communities in the south.

When a Test Seems Impossible, Get Help

Meanwhile, in order to further my skills for the demanding M.R.C.P. examination, I took yet another position to acquire more clinical experience in medicine. This was a senior internship (wow, "senior," what a big deal!) at a hospital on the outskirts of London. Life was busy because, in addition to managing inpatients, I was using available time off both to hit the books and to meet up with Jacqui.

Part one of the M.R.C.P. involved multiple-choice questions, which I surprisingly passed on my first attempt. Part two was an entirely different affair, for it required candidates to complete a "long case," an entire physical examination of a selected patient, and then report the findings to the supervising physician before making short examinations of several other patients. Later in the year, I failed this second, clinical part of the examination. I had been baffled by what I saw inside a series of patients' eyes using the ophthalmoscope. This instrument and I were not strong friends. It was tricky to maneuver quickly and see pathology inside the eyeball within the limited time allotted to examine each patient.

Given the abysmal pass rate for part two of this examination, I decided it would be wise to take the highly regarded tutorial course taught by Maurice Pappworth. The results of taking this near-legendary course were outstanding, for often it had been taken by more than half the successful M.R.C.P. candidates. I later found out that Maurice Pappworth, at the start of his career, had suffered antisemitic discrimination on multiple occasions. In a very real sense, he experienced what I feared most as a Jewish professional striving to make it in the south. On applying for a medical consultant position in 1939, he was rejected while being told that "no Jew could ever be a gentleman." Strong words, indeed! Later, after serving with distinction in World War II, he moved to London where his applications for multiple prominent medical positions were also rejected. He then resolved to turn his talents to teaching junior physicians how to tackle the difficult M.R.C.P. examination. He was widely considered to be the best teacher of internal medicine in the country, and his course was worth every penny. In hindsight, I admired his ability to carve this niche for himself and I was very grateful for his course, which would get me past a near-impossible examination.

One crucial lesson that I learned from Dr. Pappworth's course was the need to inquire of my patient for the "long case" if I had elicited all the abnormal findings on physical examination, before reporting them to the supervising physician. The curtains were drawn for this examination, so the patient and I were both hidden from sight. Nevertheless, he stressed that it was imperative to keep our voices soft. The patients were paid, year after year, for volunteering to be subjects for the examination and, he pointed out, were always on our side.

More Medical Training and More Physics I Don't Know

I had, by now, applied for a resident's position in radiology at King's College Hospital in London, which was known to be an outstanding program. I somehow squeaked into King's and was delighted to have pulled this off. There was a problem that now loomed for, while starting to learn the basics of radiology, I also needed to keep preparing for part two of the M.R.C.P by continuing to practice my clinical skills. Accordingly, I would rush off in the late afternoon to examine patients on the wards, and, while this schizophrenic approach was far from ideal, I had little choice. I do not think it helped my relationship with Jacqui, who was by now relegated to second, or even third, fiddle.

Keeping Dr. Pappworth's advice in mind, I re-took part two of the M.R.C.P. in better shape than on my first attempt. During the "long case," I quietly shared my findings with the patient. I felt proud that I had heard more than one heart murmur, especially as my hearing was not super-duper. My cardiac patient muttered something like "good boy," and then beckoned me to come closer. She whispered that I had missed an additional murmur. It was the low-pitched rumble of mitral stenosis, a critical part of her diagnosis. She pointed exactly where I needed to listen, and I was then able to faintly appreciate its sound. Ironically, it was this valve's dysfunction that had been the main cause of my late mother's death. I managed to handle the short cases satisfactorily this time, and so passed the formidable M.R.C.P. on my second go-around. What a relief this was! Now I could at last focus on radiology without the distraction of that bloody examination.

However, another hurdle now needed to be negotiated. It was physics, my old bête noire. Until we had passed the mandatory examination in physics, we were considered useless in the radiology department. The thought of learning more of this very distasteful subject was almost enough to deter me from going into radiology in the first place. As well as trying to comprehend the lectures, I had to endure the repeated trauma of physics "practicals." As should be very obvious by now, neither of these two "P's," physics and practicality, featured prominently in my skill set, so I carefully selected a partner who was very adept at mastering these seemingly purposeless laboratory exercises. I would gaze in amazement as, for three months, he deftly carried out all the requisite experiments by himself. It was all completely mystifying to me, for I had no idea what he was doing. When it came to the inevitable practical examination, I was then, of course, on my own.

Our task in the examination was to assemble a Wheatstone Bridge. To this day I cannot explain what is the purpose of a Wheatstone Bridge, nor do I care one iota. To confirm its correct assembly, we needed to see the voltmeter needle of this damned piece of equipment spring to life, moving first from left to right, then back to left and then continually repeating the process. If this happened, we knew we had made the right connections. I fiddled and fiddled, but to no avail. The invigilator walked down my aisle, and saw my attempts were not bearing fruit. Without saying a word, he turned discreetly towards me and silently pointed to two (or was it four?) wires that needed to have their connections exchanged. The next time he ventured past, the voltmeter was flickering to and fro in a very pleasing manner. He nodded his approval. It was clear that he had helped me so that I would not be a burden to him for yet another three inglorious months. I was now free to start reading X-rays and become useful in the radiology department!

You could say that I got lucky twice. A physics instructor had rescued me during the dreaded practical examination in that subject, and a kindly patient had helped me get through the monstrously difficult M.R.C.P. examination. I suppose that luck is always an ingredient in attaining one's goals, and one should not feel too guilty in taking advantage of it. After all, most people had at least one or more streaks of luck during their careers. I certainly was no exception.

Old School Radiology: Barium Studies

Work in the radiology department was quite a daunting experience. Several mornings each week, we performed barium studies on patients' gastrointestinal tracts with the assistance of technologists, all of whom were still students. The barium studies required that a white liquid be swallowed or introduced via a tube into the far end of the patient's gut, located deep between their buttocks (in case you are unaware, that's called the anus).

These barium sessions were fraught with technical errors, for we were the blind leading the blind. And we were literally in the blind, as we wore red goggles to adapt to the dark in which we were working! The exposure for the images had to be determined by novice technologists, and they were, not surprisingly, often incorrect. A barium session that was supposed to be over by lunchtime could drag on well into the afternoon, by which time we were becoming very hungry as well as worn out mentally and physically. To add to the misery, we needed to wear heavy lead aprons for radiation protection. There was no recourse to more senior radiologists for any aid, since the British system of "sink or swim" was once again the order of the day. This was very labor-intensive work, and we were never sure that the end product would be satisfactory. But it is all we had available in the pre-digital era, and so we plodded on.

Dodging Messianism and Marrying Jacqui

I was now 26 years old. Jacqui and I were married in April 1969 near her parent's home in Lindfield. It was their wish that this would be a Christian ceremony. Following in my father's footsteps, the Judaism within me was now more or less in complete recession, so I agreed to this arrangement. We had several meetings with the minister beforehand. His goal was to convert me to Christianity. I groaned at the prospect of these meetings. Each time, he explained that the path to a good life and onwards to heaven was through Jesus, and I needed to follow his teachings in order to be in touch with God. I countered by saying that I could reach God directly without first going through Jesus. He was not impressed by this straightforward logic, but neither was I impressed by his messianic efforts.

Nevertheless, despite his unsuccessful attempts, the minister agreed to marry us. He was, of course, being paid for his efforts. It was a small, lovely ceremony that took place in Jacqui's family church in Lindfield, Sussex. I am not sure what my father thought about his son being married in a church but, after all, he too had strayed far away from his flock. My atheist uncle in Israel, however, was appalled and soundly rebuked me for sealing the deal in a church. I found that to be very disturbing. My relations in the United States were relatively unaware of the event, but, knowing that they were part of an observant Jewish community, I doubt that they would have been overly thrilled. I had known Jacqui for about two years before we were married, and I was happy to now be married to her. It seemed that my transition from a Jewish background to a "non-Jewish southerner" was firmly on track. Nevertheless, I continued to feel a sense of guilt about how far I had taken such a nomadic departure from my roots.

Wedding, Jacqui and me, 1969

Ready to downhill

Father and Donnie

Luna di Miele (Honeymoon, If You—Like Me—Don't Read Italian)

For our honeymoon, we travelled to Italy, our destinations being Rome and the Amalfi coast. There was, of course, plenty to see in Rome, and Jacqui had not been there before. We arranged for a wonderful guide to take us around old Rome one day, during which she explained vividly what life was like in the Forum Romanum and the Coliseum. The gladiator's point of view was not discussed. Another day, we went to the Vatican. We even saw the Pope, though he failed to recognize us (his loss, not ours). The Vatican is an enormous palace, and we barely had time to make it to the Sistine Chapel. Michelangelo must have suffered severe neck cramps while painting the huge ceiling there, which took all of four years.

After Rome, we travelled to the Amalfi coast. There, villages were perched precariously on cliffs overlooking the plunging, spectacular coastline. We started in Sorrento, which is where the fun began. The bus that plied the coastal road from Sorrento to Amalfi could barely pass any bus coming in the opposite direction. I suppose the bus drivers were used to this, but for us this was a new and scary experience. Positano was, I think, the jewel of this coast but unfortunately had already become overrun by both artists and the super rich. Still, the plethora of tourists could not take away from its stunningly beautiful location. Amalfi was an altogether larger town, and once was an important maritime power. The beaches were small and crowded, but nevertheless afforded the opportunity to relax, sunbathe, and enjoy a great time.

On returning to London, we lived in a small apartment in an unfashionable part of South London, conveniently close to where I worked although the drive to reach the hospital took quite some time. That same year, my father and Donnie quietly tied the knot in a very small civil ceremony in Leeds. I was very happy for them. It was, all in all, quite a year!

An Important Lesson for a Young Resident

Back at work, we were now expected to grab a pile of X-ray films and read them. Before our reports were allowed to leave the department, our efforts were checked by the most senior resident. Gradually, our reports became less stupid and more meaningful. We also performed a wide variety of radiologic procedures, again without assistance. On one occasion, I tried in vain to introduce a cannula into the opening of the submandibular gland in the mouth. It was common knowledge that this opening was a very slippery noodle. After 15 or more minutes, I was still unsuccessful, so I sought the aid of our senior resident. She did not attempt the procedure herself, but instead told me to read the relevant part of a book devoted to radiologic procedures. This was quite useless, and I finally threw in both the cannula and the towel.

The head of our department was Dr. J.W. Laws, who had transformed the radiology department into one of the best in the country. He was quiet, dignified, and reserved. We all admired his integrity and his ability to hold his own with every clinician who came to our department for joint "business" conferences. One of these conferences was with Professor Roger Williams and the rather large team that worked for him. Professor Williams was an intimidating liver expert who oversaw England's first transplant of that organ.

Once, when Dr. Laws and Professor Williams were reviewing patients' X-rays, a barium study of mine popped up. The films were so dark that almost all detail was lost unless viewed with a bright light. Dr. Laws asked which one of us was responsible for this lamentable study. Reluctantly, I raised my hand to indicate ownership, whereupon Dr. Laws announced to the gathered group of 40 or so physicians that it would need to be repeated. I was crushed, but it taught me a valuable lesson; however worn out you may be, it was no excuse for sloppy work that jeopardized both the patient and the referring doctor's ability to manage their problems.

Travel, But Try to Avoid Camping: Visiting the Iberian Peninsula

In April 1970, Jacqui and I decided to go to Spain and Portugal. It was a long drive, and that meant plenty of camping. Jacqui and I argued a fair amount, and I know that my pathetic attempts to set up the tent did not help in the slightest. To be frank, I hated camping, and hated it with an unbridled passion. We had, I should explain, previously made an agreement not to have any children until we were sure that our marriage was rock solid, and the many arguments on this trip certainly did not serve to solidify our relationship. Nevertheless, we managed to have a most enjoyable holiday, stopping in two or three French towns, and then in Madrid, Granada, and Cordova.

In Madrid, we saw a bullfight, which certainly stirred the emotions. It was sad to see the inevitable end to each of the bull's lives, but the matadors themselves were clearly risking serious injury and even death. Whatever one's viewpoint, it is a cruel sport. Granada, of course, is home to the Alhambra, a magnificent Moorish palace, and the adjacent serenely peaceful Generalife gardens. The mosque cathedral at Cordova had an interesting history. It was first built by the Moors as a major center for Muslim worship. The Moors were very tolerant of Jews. While the Jews were segregated in Moorish cities, they thrived culturally and academically until the 13th century when invading Christians converted this imposing mosque into a church and, ultimately, a cathedral. We all know what happened when the Catholics took over, for everyone is only too aware of the horrors of the Spanish Inquisition. We eventually reached Lisbon, Portugal, where we stayed briefly. Our car held up for the many miles required of it and we and the vehicle returned home in good shape.

A Brief Fling with Canada

Jacqui had the wanderlust far more than me. She had spent a considerable part of her early life in colonial Malaysia, where her father was a bank manager. For her, travel had been the norm rather than the exception. She encouraged the two of us to consider working abroad. For me, this would entail considerable risk, for I had not completed my training in radiology and would need to return to England to do so. Abandonment of England for a year during training was rather like taking off for a hearty meal during a marathon race and getting lost on the way back to the course. Swanning around between different countries was not the best way to continue training in a very conservative country.

I wondered if seeking work abroad was yet another nomadic form of escape, uncertain as I still was as to whether my home was the abandoned claustrophobic world of Leeds Jewry or had now completely morphed into the more polished environs of the south. I don't think I adequately explained these confused concerns of mine to Jacqui. Even if I had, they probably would not have been foremost in her mind, for she knew where her English roots lay and that she wanted to travel abroad widely after we returned. At any rate, we tossed around the thought of taking off for Canada for a year in the middle of all my training. It was, perhaps, a compromise between our two very different goals.

All this aside, we were both excited by the idea and I decided to apply for a position in Vancouver, Canada. We knew it would be a great adventure and would give us the opportunity to explore a new and fascinating part of the world. I was, fortunately, able to obtain a one-year post at St. Paul's Hospital there. This was not the main teaching hospital in Vancouver, which added to the risk of gaining future employment in academia back home when the year was over. But it kept me connected to my training and future career and I hoped that somehow everything would work out in the long term.

While packing for our stay in Canada, Jacqui kept haranguing me to speed up my part of the process. Eventually, I had had enough of this, and left the apartment in a huff. When I arrived without Jacqui at her parents' home, they were understandably very distressed by my solo appearance and upbraided me for my thoughtlessness.

We rented an apartment high up in a skyscraper in the city's West End. From its balcony, we had an unobstructed view of the mountains of North Vancouver across the bay. Within the city of Vancouver, you could sail in the morning, and then ski in the afternoon or evening on the slopes of Grouse Mountain or Mount Seymour. Surely, it must be a contender for the city with one of the world's most spectacular settings. Its main drawback was the weather. While the summers were delightfully warm, it rained a lot in the winter. The saying went: "If it's raining on the coast, there'll be good snow in the mountains." Clearly, if you did not ski, life might be a lot less fun.

Because St. Paul's was a small hospital, professional relationships were more intimate than in my previous hospital experiences. It therefore did not take long to become acquainted with one another's foibles. Four of the five radiologists locked horns with each other all the time. Each side would explain to me the malevolent intentions of the other side. Since the head of the department, Dr. Richard Pitman, was both a superb radiologist and had a great sense of humor, I tended to align with his stars. Both he and other guy on his side, Dr. Mike Twohig, were very friendly to me. They were both British, so that may have been part of the reason. While work was clearly taken seriously, there was a much greater emphasis on outdoor activities than in England. After all, the Pacific Northwest is stunningly beautiful, with its magnetic coastline, dramatic mountain ranges, wide variety of ski resorts and beaches, as well as its many trails to hike and explore.

I had never lived in another country before coming to Canada. Obviously, it is an entirely different experience than a quick visit to a foreign country lasting just one or two weeks. Living abroad in a stunningly beautiful location only added to the experience and the excitement. Vancouver is well known for its multicultural diversity. Asians, particularly the Chinese, constitute a large percentage of its inhabitants. Despite this, there seemed to be little intermixing of the different communities. The English (or should I say British?) tended to stick together. Would you expect otherwise from a country that had rather brutally colonized so many huge swaths of the world? I think not.

We hiked, took off to nearby beaches with their scattered, windswept logs, wandered through harbors with their fishing boats and sleek-looking yachts, and enjoyed eating and strolling through Chinatown. One weekend, we took the ferry to Vancouver Island, visited the world-famous Butchart Gardens there, and took a quick spin around Victoria, the lovely and lively capital of British Columbia. Another time we travelled inland to the Okanagan Valley, sometimes considered to be a semi-desert. They actually have skiing there in the winter!

In Vancouver, we went to a rodeo. Those guys were very serious about their sport but usually did not last more than a few seconds before the bucking bronco tossed them off and left them sprawling on the ground. It was a very carefree summer and fall. My job was not demanding, and we were never lost for places to go. When winter arrived, the rains started. It seemed to us that it rained almost every day. Many times, we escaped to nearby ski resorts, including Mount Baker and Whistler Mountain. The skiing on the latter mountain was difficult, and on one trip the chair lift came to a halt in the freezing cold for 45 minutes or more. I contemplated hopping off but decided that prudence was the better part of valor and held my ground or, more exactly, my seat.

Spring came, and with it the rainfall became less incessant. Several friends suggested that we should stay here in paradise and told us that we were passing up a golden opportunity if we returned home. But I had told my father and friends that I was only going abroad for a year. I would have felt tremendous guilt if I had changed my mind. So, I applied for a position as a senior resident in Southampton and Westminster Hospital, London, with two years in each location. Obviously, I could not be interviewed face to face, and thought my chances of getting the job were slim to nonexistent. To my amazement, I found out that I had been awarded the job. I am sure the candidates back home found this to be very unsettling.

Highs and Lows: A Tour of the American West

We next organized ourselves for a long, exploratory trip of America's far west. We had come so far that to not take advantage of this immensely interesting part of the country would have been crazy. We covered a lot of ground during this trip, which introduced us to many varied and exciting locations. Wherever we went, we camped. While we saved money that way, and communed with nature, I detested the experience (as you already know). We had a full six weeks for the trip, and therefore could take our time to savor the many different sights.

Our first stop was Seattle, with its Space Needle and dramatic views of Mount Rainier away in the distance. We drove past the Olympic Mountains, and then headed south along the Oregon coast, with its miles of deserted beaches and scattered rocks out at sea known as "the stacks." In California, we saw the giant redwoods and San Francisco, drove the hair-raising, winding road of Big Sur partly enshrouded in fog, and finished up in San Diego. We crossed into Arizona, where we awoke in our tent in Monument Valley to see its dramatic rock formations as the sun was rising, and then hit the Grand Canyon.

Our last stop was Yellowstone National Park, with its gushing geysers, bison, and other wildlife. There we were in May, in the far north of the country, at an altitude of 8,000 feet. That last vital fact had completely escaped our notice, and so we were astonished to find ourselves camping between large patches of snow. As that was our last major stop, we then headed back to Vancouver.

We had one very hair-raising experience on this trip. When at the Grand Canyon, we decided to hike the Bright Angel Trail down to the Colorado River and back on the same day. Well, this hike is 17 miles in total, including an elevation change of more than 4,000 feet. The trail is narrow, and there is only one place to stop for water. Not surprisingly, you are strongly advised not to do this hike in one day, unless you make a very early start in the morning and are in good shape. We thought we fitted this latter criterion, and so we ignored the advice and did not start our descent until about 11 a.m. How foolish can you get!

We almost ran down to the Colorado River, where we happily skinny dipped, and then started back. And that is when the trouble began. Despite carrying water in our backpacks, climbing back up the path was, to put it mildly, a real ordeal. My backpack began to feel like a huge weight, and my progress was painfully slow. Jacqui handled this much better than I. Before too long, I was gulping for air and had used up most of the water that we were carrying. Towards the end of the hike, I could only walk 25 or 50 yards before stopping to catch my breath. The last mile and a half were very steep and I almost did not make it out of the canyon before nightfall. If I had not reached the top of the trail by dark, Jacqui would have needed to summon a helicopter to rescue me. Somehow, we made it back before it became too dark and dangerous. For the next two days, I lay in our tent recovering from exhaustion, dehydration, and, presumably, considerable electrolyte imbalance. Painfully, I had learned my lesson: next time, listen to the locals!

During this trip, we had the feeling that we were traveling through different countries, even though the travel was all on interstate highways once we were an hour south of Vancouver. How do you absorb so many different sceneries, climates, and cultures? The answer is: you don't, because it is so overwhelming. Massive mountain ranges, huge deserts, tightly packed cities and much else left us awestruck, enough to even give us goosebumps!

Back in Vancouver, we prepared for our return to England. We said goodbye to our Canadian friends and packed our stuff for shipping back home. We made the most of our return journey. Initially we rented a car to reach the Icefields Parkway, which stretches for 140 miles between Banff and Jasper. This route must rank as one of the most spectacular drives on earth. As we headed north out of Banff, we were soon met with stunning views of glaciers, snow-covered mountains and crystal-clear lakes. There were many places to stop along the way to get even closer to this spectacular scenery. The parkway climbed to almost 7,000 feet. Not surprisingly, it can snow there in mid-summer.

We saw at least one bear ambling across the road and managed to contain our enthusiasm for getting out of the car to extend our greetings. Just short of Jasper, we took a break and stood at the entrance to the giant Athabasca Glacier, onto which tourists could venture enclosed in an enormous vehicle. In Jasper, we boarded a sleeper train that would take us to Toronto. There is, in my opinion, nothing more boring than traveling for hour after hour past wheat and grain fields, for they are all flat, monotonous and largely indistinguishable from one another.

Our return was filled with sadness. Our goals were so different, Jacqui's main focus being to travel far and wide, while mine was to remain in England to complete my training which would take another four years. With such different paths, we agreed that it would be best if we each went our separate ways and so we divorced soon after returning to England. Jacqui recognized that completing my training, often under exacting circumstances, was essential. While I was digging into a new hospital and healthcare system in Canada, Jacqui was finding new levels of freedom and enjoyment in our travels, confirming her desire to be abroad and be as flexible as possible. Indeed, very soon after our separation, Jacqui moved to Kenya, thereby availing herself of the opportunity to travel more widely. I also think she needed a more strongly willed partner than I. As I already mentioned, I was probably too carefree and easygoing outside of work, which had been very demanding of my time. It is always a struggle to find the right balance between work and recreation.

At that age, and later, my determination to advance my career took precedence over all else. This was no different than many others in a similar situation for, even in jolly old England, the path to a good consultant job in the south was fiercely competitive and I had no desire to retreat to the north. The intent to divorce was a joint and amicable decision. We had enjoyed many great times together, and we have stayed in touch ever since. Jacqui had been a strong influence on me, and our marriage indicated that I could indeed be accepted within the southern, and non-Jewish, culture.

The Happiest Place I Ever Worked

During my training, I had many opportunities to explore different cultures and environments in short stints as locum tenens (temporary positions) in the Netherlands, in Canada, and in London. But undoubtedly, the friendliest place I worked was in Southampton. I and the other trainees worked very happily with the three general radiologists there. Every Friday afternoon, we would have a teaching session in which we were quizzed on the diagnosis of X-ray films, but this was immediately followed by our entire group retreating to a nearby pub for drinks and easy conversation, during which we would relax, laugh, and share a good number of jokes.

There was another radiologist who we greatly admired and who treated us royally. His name was Ronald Murray, and he was a world-famous musculoskeletal radiologist. He loved to teach and was a warm and enthusiastic educator. We met with him every few weeks and, as with our other consultants, would follow up a quiz session with a visit to the local pub. He regarded us benevolently as "his boys," and one time very kindly invited us to his elegant London apartment for a small party.

For this occasion, I was assigned to select the wines that would constitute our gift for his hospitality. I was no connoisseur of fine wines and needed much help in purchasing several very expensive bottles for us to take up to London. We had, as Noel Coward would say, a marvelous party. Untrained as I still was in handling more than minimal amounts of alcohol, Dr. Murray and his delightful wife raised their eyebrows in consternation at my increasingly glassy-eyed state of mind. Accordingly, they suggested that it would be prudent for me to languish overnight in their apartment before returning to Southampton. I was a little concerned about breakfast etiquette the following morning, for the Murray's lifestyle was far more exalted than mine. I managed, however, to navigate my way through the necessary maneuvers at the breakfast table and then return, sober enough to drive, to Southampton.

The contrast between this relaxed approach and the atmosphere in London to which I had been accustomed was unmistakable. In London, there was no mingling between radiologists in training and consultants, for the latter saw themselves as living on a planet far removed and loftier than those they were training. I could not help but wonder why more radiology departments and radiologists could not adopt a warmer and more civilized approach to their relationships at work. Happy folks do work harder, I would venture to say.

Learning to be Single Again

In 1972, after several months in Southampton, Jacqui and I separated. Our divorce would not become final until two years later. Allocating the items that we had collected between us did not prove difficult, as we had very few material possessions that required a decision as to who would keep what. I do remember, however, the problem we faced deciding how to divide up the two records of songs by Jacques Brel, the famous Belgian singer. After separating, we would meet on several occasions, and enjoy spending time together without any commitment hanging over our heads.

Following our separation, I moved into an apartment with a young solicitor, Alistair, and the arrangement worked out well. My belief that I had bounced back from being newly single was questioned by one girl that I dated briefly, who was studying psychology. She let me know that I had an aggressive attitude to women. I was very taken aback and adamantly disagreed. She was a fairly aggressive person herself, so I took her characterization of me with a grain of salt.

Gradually emerging into the novel world of being single, I dated two fellow health care workers, one of whom joined me in breaking the unwritten rule that you do not date anyone with whom you work closely. We were therefore extremely careful to avoid advertising our relationship. It was quite fun to see the three consultants frequently make flattering remarks about her in my presence, as they were completely unaware that we were dating. The other young lady introduced me to her mother (I think that I was expected to propose!), and on one occasion the three of us went to Glyndebourne to see "The Magic Flute," taking the customary hamper and folding table filled with delicious edibles and drinkables. It was an unforgettable experience, for I had come to love opera and an outdoor performance of this magical work by Mozart in the grounds of Glyndebourne exceeded my wildest operatic dreams.

An Overpaid Spell in the Netherlands

The opportunity to work as locum tenens in Delft, Netherlands, later arose, so for several weeks I worked there. Delft was known for both its blue pottery and as the birthplace of Vermeer. It was an attractive place, lined with fine mediaeval buildings and containing several canals. I was paid an exorbitant salary. The reason for this quickly became apparent. After performing a barium enema (a radiologic examination in which the colon is filled with barium) I was asked by the scoundrel who hired me whether I had also filled the appendix and small bowel. Not infrequently, these adjacent structures are incidentally opacified during the study. If I said "yes" to either or both these questions, he would then proceed to bill for two or three examinations, instead of just the one colon study. I have no idea how he managed to get away with this outrageous behavior.

On weekends, I travelled to Amsterdam, where I was shown around by a local who, of course, knew the city backwards. She and I had a very pleasant time together. We explored the beautiful canals, the Van Gogh Museum, and Rembrandt's house, the latter of which contained many of his famed drawings. The city was filled with young people on bicycles, which seemed to be everywhere. Although I missed out on the coffee houses of Amsterdam, where it was legal to partake of marijuana, I loved the ambiance of the city, where tradition and modernity so clearly complimented each other.

Still the Country Bumpkin

When I finished my two years in Southampton, I moved back up to London for the second half of my senior residency in radiology. The other trainees were based in London at Westminster Hospital for all four years, so, having been in Southampton for the first two years, I felt like a country bumpkin. The department was rather stuffy, and there were insufficient X-rays to keep us all fully occupied. Westminster was a relatively small teaching hospital. One of its main functions, I was humorously informed, was to handle any medical complications of drunk members of the nearby Houses of Parliament and Lords, often incurred by falling and injuring themselves in the process.

For my two years back in London, I stayed in Putney in an oddly configured dwelling that apparently resulted from the conversion of an old horse barn into habitation for humans. The bath was behind a screen in the kitchen, and the toilet was outside. My dwelling mate was Deirdre Ridsdell-Smith, a friend of Jacqui's. Deirdre was amused by what she considered to be my dating routine: the first date was a drink and maybe a film, the second a dinner, and the third, if there was to be a third, a visit to the opera. I have no recollection of this apparent protocol, so I will have to take her word for it. Her social life was decidedly less mainstream than mine. She had spent some time in San Francisco leading a carefree hippie lifestyle, which continued in an attenuated form when she returned to London. She had a sweet, lively manner and, not surprisingly, had a variety of unconventional boyfriends. We got on well together, each leading our own very different lives.

The combination of my one-year fling in Canada and my time in non-opulent Southampton was not exactly encouraging for the prospects of subsequently obtaining a consultant job in the south, where the perception of pedigree exceeded all other parameters of qualification. The feeling that I did not belong once again haunted me, but there was little that I could do about it. I was also the only resident assigned to work in the London suburb of Roehampton, which was not exactly on a par to being nearby the Houses of Parliament and Lords. In Roehampton, I discovered that my old school friend, Michael Cooke, was working in the dental department, and I really enjoyed re-connecting with him. We had failed to stay in touch during my years with Jacqui and I had the impression that he was uncomfortable with my conversion to the smoother southern way of life, since he had unabashedly retained a down-to-earth approach, based on his northern roots.

What's Crazy about Crete?

We were two friends in Crete, Tony and me. Actually three, for Tony's friend Dick was also there. Tony and Dick were a hoot and kept us in stitches all the time. I was now in my late twenties and, like so many North Europeans, very ready for the Mediterranean sun. Together, we three rented a robust car for Crete's rocky roads, with the palace of Knossos high on the agenda. Of course, Knossos was the home of Minos, the famed mythical king of Crete. I was not at all enamored by its rubble, but Dick was a classics scholar so I played unwilling tagalong.

There were better times in store, with days on sun-kissed beaches, and wild Greek restaurants to keep us occupied in the evenings. The Greek waiters were a dazzling collection of guys, and full well knew it. While dancing, they gracefully swung their legs over our heads, picked up tables with their teeth (!), and shattered food-less plates. They were also very handsome which, together with these antics, guaranteed the attention of otherwise restrained young female tourists.

Back in London, Tony, I, and his friends would cruise the Thames in his gin tub boat, party and generally have a good time. It was not until later that his life took a more serious turn. He became a very successful shipping lawyer and married Gabrijela, who was the daughter of a Croatian shipping magnate. They had a rather refined home in Hampstead, London, in which he once proudly showed me a Rembrandt (although admittedly a rather small piece).

His backyard contained a grass tennis court on which he and the Croatian ambassador to England would play from time to time. One weekend that I stayed with Tony and Gabrijela, they received a dinner invitation to the Croatian ambassador's residence and managed to have me included. The Croatian ambassador was surrounded by his diplomatic corps. As you well know, I have Serbian relations, so, knowing there was no love lost between Serbs and Croatians, I decided, at least during dinner, to keep my mouth shut.

After dinner, the ambassador took me into his library. I asked him if he had read "Balkan Ghosts" by Robert Kaplan, which he knew was not at all complimentary to the Croatians and the atrocities they committed during World War II. The ambassador said the book was all nonsense, and he suggested two other books that would serve to straighten me out on Croatian and Serbian issues. History, of course, has always varied, and will always vary, with its storyteller. I dutifully noted the names of the two books but tore up the scrap of paper immediately on my return to Tony's.

But back to Crete. That is where I had first met Tony. We were both dipping our toes in the sea and had started chatting. As we talked and exchanged information, he said that he had been invited to my parent's home in Leeds where he had attended law school. "Nonsense," I replied. It turned out that our late mothers had been the closest of school friends in Klagenfurt, Austria. It was that contact that had led him to visit my parent's home. Meanwhile, I was in medical school in London, his hometown, so our paths had never crossed! That is what's so crazy about Crete, where a completely unforeseen coincidence took place! How often does this kind of thing happen?

A FORTUITOUS CONNECTION

While doing another locum tenens, this time for my friend Noel Blake in Dublin, Eire, I happened to have coffee with an Irish expatriate from

Canada. I expressed a desire to return to Canada when I had concluded my training in England, and to obtain a consultant's position there in one of its three big cities: Vancouver, Toronto, or Montreal. Sadly, he informed me that Canada had enough radiologists of its own and would only hire those few from abroad who had already established an outstanding research reputation in a field that Canada sorely needed. Research reputation? There was nothing in my resume about any such activities, so that idea could be entirely erased from my mind.

This news made me disconsolate, whereupon I commented that perhaps I would try to obtain a position in the United States. There, medical practice was almost the polar opposite of that in England, the emphasis being on lucrative private practice rather than a socialized system of medicine. When my coffee companion wrote the name of a radiologist, Dr. Robert McLelland at Duke University Medical Center, on a scrap of paper, I kept this in my possession. Back in London, I asked the head of the radiology department at Westminster Hospital if he would act as a reference for my applications to well-known university medical centers in the United States, to which he readily agreed. At the same time, I wrote to Dr. McLelland at Duke Medical Center in the USA, even though his primary role was to organize continuing medical education programs rather than recruit staff. I have always been of the opinion that, if the door is only a few inches open, why not give it a kick and see what happens. There is nothing to lose, and much that may be gained. It is an approach that I later thoroughly ingrained in our children.

Hitting Club Med and Trying Weed (You know...The Doctor Stuff)

There was one radiologist, Paul Frank, at Westminster Hospital with whom I had become friendly. We decided to take a Club Mediterranean (Club Med) vacation together. A basic premise of all Club Med vacations is that you never need to leave the premises, for everything you might need for a relaxed holiday is on site. In those days, Club Med either catered to families or singles, clearly two markets with very different flavors. Paul and I chose, not surprisingly, the singles flavor. Our destination was the French Caribbean island of Martinique.

On the flight there, I engaged in lively conversation with a female co-traveler and we agreed to spend time together after we had arrived at the resort. If you were a guest at Club Med, you were designated as one of the "Gentils Members" (GMs), in contrast to the staff who were referred to as "Gentils Organisateurs" (GOs). The GOs were, without exception, both worldly and charming. A prerequisite for them to be hired was that they needed to be exceedingly good looking. The disc jockey there had all these qualities in spades. Consequently, each evening a steady stream of female GMs would gawk hungrily at his antics, and he became a revolving door for sophisticated seduction. The girl I had met on the way down was one of his many conquests.

I spoke to the head GO there, expressing my thoughts about the GO's dubious dual roles, and he assured me that amorous evenings and nights with them were a deliberate part of the program. That, then, was the end of my potential romance. On the way back, several of us vacationing at the resort were invited to the Miami apartment of a social worker who had also been at Club Med. We were given weed, and I remember listening to music while lying under a coffee table there. I had never heard such amazing sounds in my life. It was an unforgettable experience. I was subsequently able to partake of more weed in the United States, and I unashamedly loved the stuff. Under controlled circumstances, bring it on, s'il vous plait!

Interlude: Did a Relation of Mine Invent the First Car?

Yes, indeed! I have a distant relation on my paternal grandmother's side who was a prolific inventor named Siegfried Marcus and was, of course, Jewish. He was born in 1831, and died in 1898, the same year, incidentally, that Adolf Hitler was born. According to Wikipedia, Marcus is credited with having invented the petrol-driven motor car. The vehicle he designed had four wheels, a steering wheel and a sophisticated electrical system.

Why was Marcus's invention not recognized? It was because the Nazis did not want anyone to know about it. Hitler's favorite car was the Mercedes-Benz, and he gave his support and many contracts to that company. Mercedes-Benz claimed to have been the first to invent the car, but their device was much cruder. Goebbel's propaganda ministry sent explicit instructions to the editors of the Austrian encyclopedia to delete any reference to Marcus's achievement, and removed his distinguished grave, his statue, and commemorative plaques. Nazi thugs were sent with sledgehammers to destroy his car, which stood in a museum. However, the curators had been tipped off about this, and buried the car underground.

In 1950, the vehicle was unearthed and put to the test. It worked! Mercedes-Benz, however, has declined to respond to inquiries about the controversy. It would, of course, be bad for their world-wide, luxury brand, business, and would reveal their widespread and willing collaboration with the Nazi party before and during World War II. However, Marcus did belatedly receive a measure of respect. He was re-interred in an honorary tomb in Vienna, and a statue of him placed in front of the Technical University. May his memory and achievement live forever!

WAITING FOR SOMEONE TO RETIRE OR DIE

After passing boards in radiology (the F.R.C.R. i.e., Fellow of the Royal College of Radiologists) it was now time to start looking for a consultant's post. New positions were rarely created in the cash-strapped National Health Service, so one had to wait for someone to retire or die. The latter was somewhat difficult to predict, so we all looked for posts in which the incumbent was retiring. Somehow, the grapevine told us which of these positions would be opening up. There were very few decent jobs that would be available in the south, and far too many candidates applying for them. I tried for a job in Croydon, a town about one hour south of London. One of the interviewers questioned me about all the moves I had made during my training and informed me: "We can't hire you. You're too much of a wanderer." It was immaterial, because the position had already been filled, and all the interviews were meaningless.

With no other respectable positions in the south that I, with my here, there and everywhere credentials, could expect to obtain, I reluctantly considered a job in Manchester. This would take me back, of course, to the north of England. The post was a university position but not the main university in that city. I interviewed there, and the interview went well because there was a very strong department of gastroenterology, and I was able to express my growing interest in radiologic studies of the stomach. I remember taking the train back to London and feeling despondent about returning to the north, with my tail between my legs.

And then something amazing happened. I received a phone call from the vice chairman of the radiology department at Duke University Medical Center, offering me a position there for $36,000 per year, far more than any National Health Service position would be paying. Not only that, but I could choose in which areas to work. This all seemed too good to be true! And all this through a name written on a napkin in a coffee shop in Dublin. Even though Duke was in the middle of nowhere in the American south, it appeared to have a good reputation, so I took the job. Meanwhile, Paul Frank had taken a position at Northwestern University, Chicago, located on the city's lakefront, and I was mighty jealous!

Deirdre and I organized a farewell party. I remember lying on my back in the garden, looking up at the sky and dreaming. Saying goodbye to all my friends was, obviously, hard, as was shaving off my beard, for such a large collection of facial hair would not fare well in the torrid heat of North Carolina. It must have been a very difficult pill for my father to swallow, with his only son taking off for a faraway country. He was, however, very understanding, and realized that the opportunities would be far greater in the states than in England.

I was under the impression that, in the states, there was no need to wait for someone to retire or die, and that you could just pick up the phone and see what's cooking elsewhere. I had the feeling that I would never return to England and its old-fashioned class-conscious way of life. Nevertheless, it was not at all clear to me what to expect when I arrived.

There I was, after 14 years of training, jumping off into the relative unknown. Even if I had no friends in the United States, at least I had family on my mother's side in the American Northeast. Many other physicians left England in 1975, for the Minister of Health was threatening to abolish all private beds in the National Health Service, and opportunities for private practice were still few and far between. Socialism was about to be, to the best of our knowledge, carried too far, and I had no wish to be caught up in the process!

Part Four

ONTO THE USA:
NORTH CAROLINA

An Englishman in North Carolina

Moving from Leeds to England's south was a big step for me, but this cultural and societal change was dwarfed by my move to the United States. I felt as if I had been spirited into an altogether different world, and even a different planet. It was not at all clear to me what to expect when I arrived. My identity was now even more precarious, especially as Duke University was located in the American south, notorious for its backwardness and unrelenting racial intolerance. Only six years earlier, there had been violent race riots about 90 minutes away in Greensboro.

Duke University, as it turned out, was not at all backward, but if you drove 10 miles or so into the surrounding countryside, you could see roadside signposts filled with bullet holes. Even more alarming, when you travelled through North Carolina to its eastern coast, you passed through a town named Smithfield, on the outskirts of which a large billboard proudly welcomed you to Ku Klux Klan country. Years later, a radiologist friend suggested that I look at a position in a large hospital in Metairie, Louisiana. I declined the opportunity, feeling that Louisiana was too far into the deep south for me to venture. This fear was born out when David Duke, an ex-grand wizard of the KKK, a strong antisemite and an ardent fan of Hitler, was appointed to the state legislature of Louisiana by the all-white voters of Metairie in 1989.

Duke University, located in Durham, was one of three universities that constituted the Research Triangle area. The others were the University of North Carolina and North Carolina State University. As such, the prevailing atmosphere there had very little in common with the deeply discriminatory attitudes in many other parts of the south. Most of my friends were either MDs or Ph.D.s and there was very little interaction with the local population. "Town and gown" were clearly social divisions that were very much separated from each other, despite their close proximity.

In July, the average high temperature in North Carolina is 88 degrees, but that does not tell the real story. When you take the humidity into consideration, it is a totally different ballgame. The average humidity there in July is 88 percent, making it 106 degrees according to the heat index. Even after 45 years in the states, I still have not acclimatized to this. When I arrived in North Carolina in mid-summer, I was hoping to play some tennis. Because of the oppressive heat, I deferred playing this sport for six or more weeks. I then played in the late evening. After one set, I felt like I had gone down with a bad case of the flu and threw myself, fully dressed except for my shoes, into the faculty pool in order to resuscitate myself.

Needing a car, I bought a Toyota Corolla for $3,000. This was a good buy for, after owning it for 10 years, maintaining it had never cost more than $100 a year. Those were clearly different times! For a while, I stayed in Duke's International House but obviously needed to find a place of my own. After looking around, I found an apartment in nearby Chapel Hill that backed up onto the local country club's golf course.

In one unavoidably memorable moment during a bout of severe diarrhea, I recall turning the lights out in the apartment and retiring to bed at the unusual hour of eight in the evening only for my sleep to be disturbed by a rustling sound. That sound was getting louder and closer, and instinctively, without any pretensions towards heroism, I yelled: "Get out!" After waiting a minute or so, I gingerly made my way downstairs. The intruder had fled, apparently without taking any major items. I immediately called the police, who said they would be there quickly, but in my breathless summary of the event, the diarrhea that had prematurely sent me to bed suddenly returned with a vengeance. I barely had time to clean myself up in the shower before the police arrived. The moral of this story is, perhaps, that one should not live in a building whose windows or back door are so obviously available to intruders. For several months afterwards, I kept a sand wedge at my bedside. If there was to be a repeat episode, I could at least throw it in the approximate direction of any uninvited guest.

Daily work in the radiology department started at 7:30 in the morning, drastically different to my experience in London. There, we rolled up our sleeves at 9:15 or so, after having a much-needed coffee to revive ourselves after the crazy drive across the city to the hospital. It seemed to me that 8:15 represented a very reasonable compromise, so that is when I chose to start work. After almost a year, I was advised that this was, in fact, unacceptable. I'm not sure why they waited so long to inform me! Anyway, I had little choice but to acquiesce. I was also asked if I could perform the barium studies wearing shoes instead of just socks. This seemed unnecessary since we were carrying out the examinations in total darkness, but there was little to be gained by debating this.

I had a variety of girlfriends, but no meaningful relationships developed from these situations and this aspect of my life seemed rather superficial. It was as if I was making up for lost time from those early days before meeting Jacqui who was, in fact, my first serious girlfriend. Given the need to devote increasing time to the "publish or perish" mode of existence at Duke, maintaining an intense relationship would likely have been very demanding. As Dame Margot Fonteyn, at one time the world's leading ballerina, famously said: "The one important thing I learned over the years is the difference between taking one's work seriously and taking one's self seriously. The first is imperative and the second disastrous."

Overall, in my first few months in the United States, I found myself hot, well-shoed, and ready to defend against any manner of invasion of my living quarters. Chapel Hill was a delightful university town, quite unlike Durham, which was very southern and tobacco-based. Looking back, adapting to this new environment early on was a somewhat disorienting experience. Nomads have to take whatever comes their way, of course, for otherwise they need to keep moving on.

Continuing My Impressive Tennis Career

Social life revolved mainly around friends in the Radiology Department and the Faculty Club with its most welcome swimming pool and tennis courts. I decided that four or more hours on a golf course in the height of the summer was more than I could handle, whereas a relatively short game of tennis early in the day would ultimately become manageable. I met several folks at the Duke Faculty Club, and became particularly friendly with Jeff Collins and his girlfriend, Rose Mills. Jeff and I played a lot of tennis together, hoping to conclude the proceedings before it became too hot. That did not always happen, but there was no quitting until one of us had downed the other.

Another aspect of tennis happened in a surprising way. After a year at Duke, I was placed in charge of medical students who had chosen to spend a month in the Radiology Department. This was no honor, because the mantra at the institution was research, teaching and patient care, and in THAT order. Furthermore, teaching medical students was considered far less important than teaching our own radiology residents. Once a year, there was a "round robin" tennis tournament involving faculty and medical students, a tradition that had been instituted by the head of the medical center, Bill Anlyan. Despite the fact that he had ankylosing spondylitis and could only serve underhand with his hunched up body frame, he was very dedicated to the game. His underhand serve had a wicked twist to it, which could sometimes outfox even the best of players.

One year, a medical student who wanted to pursue radiology as a career approached me to be his partner for this annual "round robin." Clearly, he sought me out because he wanted a strong reference from me. I agreed to partner him, but only after learning that he had previously played in the Davis Cup for Israel. How could I pass up an opportunity like this? In our games, he told me to take care of one tramline and that he would cover the rest of our side of the court. Naturally, I obeyed these instructions. There was much concern that his line calls were dubious, but there was no way that I could ever have known as the ball was flying around so fast. We won the "round robin," the only time I ever won a tennis event. I was, needless to say, thrilled. He did get a reference from me, but I was careful not to exaggerate his prowess in matters related to radiology.

American Immigration: A System That Could Never Be More Absurd

I came to the United States on a temporary visa since it was the only way that I could arrive in time to start working at the beginning of the academic year on July 1. At the end of this first year at Duke, I went to the state licensing board to renew my visa. The first question tossed my way by the idiot behind his desk (in a recorded interview, no less) was an inquiry as to whether I was, or had ever been, a member of the Communist Party. I was rather stunned by this, as I thought that the Joe McCarthy era was long since over. The guy informed me that my visa was only temporary, and this raised a serious problem about extending my stay in the country. I explained that I had no intention of returning to England, but this did not seem to have any effect on him. Reluctantly, he extended my visa but warned me that I might have to leave the country for two years before I could apply for the green card that would make me a permanent resident. Fortunately, my uncle Hermann was an immigration attorney. I contacted him almost immediately after this discouraging experience and, luckily, he was able to expedite converting my temporary status to one of permanence.

After Hermann had prepared the ground, I needed to have an interview to formally obtain my green card. The nearest immigration service offices were located about five hours away in Norfolk, Virginia. I arrived for my appointment and waited patiently for this crucial interview in a large room filled mainly, it appeared, with people from Central America. Finally, I was ushered into the interview room. The guy behind the desk looked at my papers, saw that I was on the Duke Faculty and asked me, at most, two questions. That left about 20 minutes or so of remaining interview time. He looked me straight in the eye and asked if I knew why men went to war. I thought this to be a very odd question. I responded that, often, they sought more land or perhaps wanted to convert neighboring countries to their religion and culture. He then said that he would explain to me the "true reason" for declaring war and proceeded to inquire whether I had always experienced sufficient relationships with women. Now, the interview was clearly taking an even more bizarre turn.

My reply about relationships with women was, hesitatingly, along the lines of "sometimes yes, and sometimes no." He then proceeded to give me his thoughts about declarations of war. These centered around the fact that, usually, those who died in a war were not the leaders but the male troops serving under them. He went on to explain that leaders went to war so that there would be proportionately more women available to them after the battlefield losses of so many of the troops' lives.

He next asked me if I could get him invited to Duke so that he could address the student body about this crackpot theory. I said that I had very little contact or influence with undergraduates but, since I still needed his signature for obtaining the green card, I would try my best; a whopping lie, of course, as I had no intention of doing so. He then sat back in his chair, signed the form for the green card, and I breathed a sigh of relief. I concluded that there are nutcases working both for the licensing boards and the immigration services and drove home puzzled and scratching my head all the way.

It was not until 14 or so years later that I finally applied for citizenship, for there seemed no urgency at all to do this. I suppose that I did not feel particularly American and, while life here was far more opportunistic than back in England, the United States certainly had its own set of issues. A very capitalistic society that paid scant attention to the poor, and tolerated considerable racial injustice, was still the order of the day. Furthermore, my adopted country certainly had more than its fair share of wackos, probably as a result of the freedom available to all. Yet, I was not complaining, since life here was definitely better when compared to England's stuffiness and rigid class system.

However, the statement that life is better in the United States is true only if you are not a person of color. White supremacy had always been a very strong force in this country, and there are probably many who have happily long subscribed to this form of racism but have remained conveniently quiet on the issue. In the UK, racism is more directed to foreigners of all kinds rather than to blacks specifically. Furthermore, there has never been legal segregation in the UK. Both countries, of course, were complicit in the slave trade, but the economic success of the USA, unlike in the UK, was only made possible because it was developed on the backs of slaves. Racism, I concluded, had been — and still was — far more overt in this country, unfortunately.

Living in White Christian Academia

The only discernible social structure that impinged on me was that of the Duke faculty, almost all of whom were married. I was the exception to the rule. Both Reed Rice, my mentor, and Herman Grossman, a pediatric radiologist who had also become a good friend, set me up on one or two blind dates, which I certainly appreciated. However, most of the time I had to do my own searching, and this usually took place in nearby Chapel Hill.

Very few of the African Americans outside the university setting were treated with any respect. I remember when the Duke Radiology Department hosted a continuing medical education course at the "whites only" Hope Valley Country Club, often referred to as Hopeless Valley. Several black radiologists attended the course, which took place in one of the club's private rooms. This led to Robert McLelland, who was both a member of the club and ran the postgraduate course, being hauled in for questioning, only to be told that, if he ever brought another black guest there, his membership would be summarily terminated.

When I had been at Duke for a couple of years, the university held a symposium focused on the Holocaust. The featured speaker was Elie Wiesel, the noted author and humanitarian who had survived both the Auschwitz and Buchenwald concentration camps. He was, of course, a legendary figure. I remember another speaker, Franklin Littell, who was both a Protestant minister and a celebrated professor, roundly criticizing Christian antisemitism, which he accused of having laid the groundwork for Nazi inhumanity. He explicitly stated that, unless Christians sincerely admit their longstanding historic guilt, there would never be any meaningful dialogue between Jews and Christians.

At the time, I was happily dating a vivacious Catholic lady who taught in the radiology program at the nearby Department of Veterans Affairs hospital.

However, when I brought up the subject of Christian guilt, she responded that this was not a subject of particular concern to her. I immediately realized that developing the relationship further would be a betrayal of my background, and therefore, after further attempts to extract a measure of empathy from her, we parted ways. Even though I was living in a non-Jewish world, this was more than I could reasonably tolerate.

A Uniquely American Tradition: NCAA Basketball

One benefit of being at Duke was having the opportunity to obtain basketball tickets. When I arrived, Duke was arguably the worst team in the Atlantic Coast Conference and possessed only one good player, Jim Spanarkel. It was therefore a piece of cake to get season tickets to their games. This all changed within the next year or two when Duke made the basketball finals of the National Collegiate Athletic Association (NCAA). Mike Krzyzewski, or "Coach K," became head coach in 1980, and it was soon after his arrival that the team became and remained a feared powerhouse of players. Coach K was to become the winningest coach in the NCAA, with more than 1,200 wins and five NCAA championships.

The rivalry between Duke University and the University of North Carolina was particularly intense. For a spectator sport, these local derbies were without parallel. Duke fans were famous for yelling relentless abuse at many of the visiting teams. North Carolina State had a series of players who committed increasingly unacceptable misdemeanors. When they were in possession of the ball, Duke's students would loudly chant en masse: "If you can't go to school, go to State," followed by: "If you can't go to State, go to jail." On several occasions, the Duke coach had to make a public appeal to the students to back off from delivering such reverberating verbal taunts.

It was easy to get caught up in college sports, for they are huge business in this country. When the new head coach of the University of Texas was hired last year, he was guaranteed $34 million in base pay over the next six years. In contrast, a Nobel Prize-winning physicist at the same university earns approximately one tenth of this amount per year. Doesn't that say it all about the crazy dominance of college sports in the USA?

SGR: The Society of "Super Great Radiologists"

I joined the Society of Gastrointestinal Radiologists (SGR) soon after arriving in this country. Their annual meetings always took place in beautiful locations such as Maui, Banff Springs and Palm Beach. All the resorts, it should be noted, boasted attractive golf courses, many tennis courts, swimming pools and delicious but very expensive food. The first that I attended was on Hilton Head Island. On the way down, I decided that South Carolina's main sources of income must be guns and fireworks and, on entering the tourist-infested island, saw the crowded slums housing large numbers of African Americans. Once beyond this area, nearly everyone holidaying on the island was white. Clearly, the black workers formed the basis for the island's service industries.

Between the talks given at the meeting, the radiologists gathered, large drinks in hand, around one of the hotel's magnificent pools. There, to my amazement, I found myself in conversation with famous radiologists casually dressed in shorts and T-shirts. This would never have happened in England. The openness of American society, albeit essentially white, took a little time to get used to. At the meeting, I realized how lucky I was to hang out with legendary radiologists in such a relaxed atmosphere. At these meetings, the SGR always arranged a tennis tournament, a golf tournament, as well as sundry other activities. Life in this super great society felt good, and it seemed that it would only get better as I came to know more of its members over succeeding years.

As the years rolled by, it became obvious that a subset of the younger radiologists would dance, drink, and cavort around into the early hours of the morning. Since I left this increasingly wild scene at a relatively early hour, I can only guess as to what transpired later on. The word was out that not everyone found their own room to sleep off their increasingly disoriented and intoxicated state.

Opera was not her Cup of Tea

One afternoon, for the first time, I decided to run laps in the Duke University gym next to the basketball stadium. While indulging in this activity, I could not help but notice an attractive young lady conversing with a faculty member of the radiation therapy department. I only vaguely knew him, but that certainly was not going to stop me from approaching the two of them and engaging in some meaningless banter. The young lady was wearing a short white coat, really a jacket, and I did not know what this indicated within the medical hierarchy. Afterwards, I found out that short white coats were worn by physician assistants. The problem now was to find out how to contact her, knowing only her first name. Somehow, I overcame this hurdle, phoning her and asking if she would like to see an opera by Mozart, "Cosi fan Tutte," which, roughly translated, means "They (women) are all like that." Anne was the young lady's name, and she may have had a hard time understanding my English accent, but, more importantly, she informed me that she did not like opera at all.

Despite this rejection, it seemed that she had left the door slightly open so I phoned a second time in an attempt to engage her in some other activity. In this way, our first date became a game of tennis. We were fairly equally matched. Her all-round game was better, but I had a serve which, if working, could do some damage. Following this we went out for dinner to a restaurant I asked Anne to suggest, being the gentleman that I am. As Anne remembers, I commented afterwards that it was quite expensive, which she promptly filed away as information worth knowing.

We dated with increasing frequency and shared many wonderful times together. One early date was a surprise birthday party for the wife of David Paletz, a noted faculty professor who taught political communication (whatever that is, I still do not know). His wife Darcy had worked in the film industry in Hollywood, and to celebrate her birthday we were all expected to dress as MGM film characters. I remember that we went to the local pharmacy, where I covered my belly with an expansile device to mimic Oliver Hardy, while Anne had the easier job of playing Stan Laurel. Even though we knew very few people there, it was great fun.

We frequently went to the North Carolina coast, usually with Jeff and his girlfriend Rose. A side benefit of this was his offer of weed, which I gratefully accepted. It had a positive effect on me but seemed to have none on Anne. We also went to Washington, D.C., a new experience for both of us. These were very happy times, carefree and full of fun. On one occasion, I was invited to a party that was thrown by Anne's friends. I arrived rather late, to Anne's consternation, and then proceeded to dance somewhat out of control around my umbrella. I thought this to be exceedingly funny, but this sentiment did not seem to be widely shared.

As I mentioned, Anne was a physician assistant (PA) at Duke, which founded the PA system that was later to spread across the country. Physician assistants worked in conjunction with physicians to both diagnose and carry out treatments after a rigorous three-year training period. In remote areas of the country, they were often the only providers of health care, which required taking much more responsibility than just working closely alongside a physician. Anne was working as a PA at Duke for a gastroenterologist, John Garbutt, with whom I had frequent contact since I read the X-rays of many of his patients.

Marrying Anne and Learning I'm not Considered a Jew

I was on cloud nine. Despite our different backgrounds, we had much in common. Medicine was a strong bond, and that mattered to Anne since her father and many of her relatives were physicians. We loved to play tennis, go to the beach and, despite her reluctance to hear opera, we enjoyed many great times together. I clearly knew that I wanted to marry her. As with Jacqui, I did not follow the time-honored convention of asking Anne's father for consent to marry his daughter. My proposal was not a carefully created moment in a romantic setting, for it took place at the airport as Anne was leaving to spend Christmas with her parents and family. When she informed them that we intended to become husband and wife, they accepted this news despite preferring that their daughter married a Christian. I could understand this. They were from Evansville, Indiana, an area that did not seem to greatly embrace diversity. Interestingly, though, Anne's mother's best friend was Jewish. And Anne's parents, Bill and Sally, were always very warm and welcoming whenever we all spent time together.

Now we needed to find a person of faith who would marry us. When Jacqui and I were married by a Methodist minister, my atheist uncle in Israel had given me a very hard time about failing to have a Jewish ceremony. So, this time, I determined that we should be married by a rabbi. This was not that simple, for we could not find a rabbi in our vicinity who was prepared to marry two people of differing faiths. Finally, we found a Reform rabbi in Raleigh, about 30 minutes away, who agreed to perform the ceremony. First, though, we were to meet with him three or four times.

After inquiring about my religious observance and realizing that there was essentially no Jewish ritual in my life, he announced that, in his eyes, I was not considered Jewish. It seemed to me that he took the narrow definition of a Jew as one who practiced the rituals of the faith, rather than the broader definition of someone whose ancestors are descended from the ancient tribes of Israel. Hitler's definition of a Jew, according to the Nuremberg Laws, was someone who had at least three Jewish grandparents, irrespective of their religious practice. I was rather alarmed by the rabbi's refusal to acknowledge my Jewishness. As that definition resulted in the death of six million Jews, I would have almost certainly perished if my parents had stayed in Austria. Therefore, I argued, if that definition was good enough for Hitler, it was also good enough for me. Who was the rabbi to say that I was not Jewish based on my irreligiosity? He agreed to marry us, but not before trying to persuade me to adopt religious practices.

I found it ironic that the minister who married Jacqui and me considered me to be a Jew, and therefore ripe for conversion to Christianity, but this rabbi did not. If both of these men were correct, then what the hell was I? And why were these religious leaders adopting such radically different perspectives about my racial/religious identity?

Our wedding took place outdoors in sweltering heat in Duke Gardens, which did not interfere with the happiness of the occasion. Anne looked radiantly lovely. The ceremony was low key, and the rabbi avoided playing any religious cards too strongly. The reception was in the elegantly old-fashioned Villa Teo that served European-style food in a lovely Italianate setting. Interestingly, persuading my two surviving American uncles in the northeast to travel as far south as North Carolina, not exactly Jewish territory, was an exceedingly difficult task, but they finally agreed to make the journey. I think that my marriage to a non-Jewish woman was a strong factor in inclining them not to come, for they lived in an almost exclusively Jewish society. Anne's cousins came, as well as Miriam, one of my cousins. My father and Donnie, of course, flew over for the occasion, and it was lovely to be all together again.

HONEYMOON

For our honeymoon, I kept Anne in the dark as to our destination but did suggest that attire for a warm climate would be highly appropriate. We spent our first married night at the luxurious Plaza Hotel just south of Central Park in New York City. When we headed to the airport and boarded our plane, the advertised stops were Barbados, St. Vincent, and Trinidad. As the plane dipped down for its first landing, Barbados, Anne thought this was our likely destination since the island was a noted tourist destination. "No," I said, "this is not for us." The next stop was St. Vincent and, as the plane started its descent, a very small island just south of St. Vincent came into view. This was Young Island, and this was where we would be staying.

Young Island was accessed by a very short boat ride. One day we swam from Young Island to the mainland and back without any difficulty. To be honest, it was only 200 yards each way! The resort occupied the entire small island and was very low key and unspoiled. The accommodations were cottages, surrounded by lush tropical vegetation. We took our showers in privacy outdoors, had delicious meals, enjoyed its lovely beach accompanied by mouth-watering rum punches, played some tennis on a court that had known better days, and wandered all over the hilly property.

One day, we went to St. Vincent and visited the Spice Garden, where it seemed that every spice tree and plant on earth was growing. Our guide told us what spice we were tasting or sniffing as we made our way around these fascinating plants and trees. Another day we took a trip to sleepy Bequia, an island without traffic or fancy resorts, and where all the families were connected to the sea by boatbuilding, fishing, whaling, or other seafaring activities. Walking around Bequia, we felt that it was a place where time had stood still, and everything was delightfully undisturbed. After such a relaxing and romantic stay in the area, we were both loathe to return to so-called civilization.

With our marriage, our circle of friends broadened. Most, but not all, were Jewish. Despite this, my skepticism of the Jewish tradition remained strong, and I persisted in giving vent to my strong concerns about Jewish religion and Jewish society at large. Without exception, our friends were still M.D.s or Ph.D.s. The atmosphere was fun, but, shall I say, just slightly rarified.

MATURING IN MY PROFESSION

It should be obvious by now that I was never a scientist. Nevertheless, I was able to give many talks about radiology of the large bowel using the double contrast approach. I'll spare you the cumbersome details of what "double contrast" means, for why should you care? This emerging technique was still relatively unused in the United States, and so was fertile ground for me to discuss. I also suspect that my English accent helped to create a distinctive air to which Americans were susceptible.

Wedding, Anne and me, 1979

Father and me

Anne, Elizabeth, David, and me, 1988

Three generations, with Anne's mother, Sally, and father, Bill

I was starting to be invited to be a visiting professor at other institutions. This led to offers to join the faculty at New York-Presbyterian/Columbia University Hospital in New York City, Northwestern Memorial Hospital in Chicago, and several other prestigious institutions. I turned them all down not only because living in these cities seemed to require long commutes but also because I knew that I could not lead a section and stimulate research if I was not a true scientist.

Nevertheless, once I became a player on the lecture circuit, it was easy to be seduced into staying on this hamster wheel. Almost no young radiologist in his right mind would shy away from these opportunities. This was especially true at Duke, where the environment was transformed into a highly competitive one following the arrival of Charles Putman from Yale as its new chairman.

Time to Leave my Funky House

After two years, Herman Grossman and Reed Rice encouraged me to buy a house rather than continuing to rent the apartment on the golf course. I bought a house deep in the trees that ensured essentially total privacy and became very attached to it.

Subsequently, Anne and her mother Sally felt strongly that my weird tree house was too small for a couple. Incidentally, they informed me that the rooms were knee deep in dust particles, of which I was completely oblivious. Anne had many allergies, and house dust almost certainly qualified as one of the main offenders.

One day, Anne and Sally went for a walk in the neighborhood, and returned to tell me about a house they had seen that was four times the cost of my cozy, quixotic home. I was very taken aback. Fortunately, this potential relocation was not pursued. Instead, we built a fairly large house in a nearby neighborhood in Chapel Hill. The foreman had a reputation for bullying women. I explained that Anne would oversee all decisions relating to the construction. She could look at a floor plan and it made immediate sense to her, whereas I was completely unable to imagine what the construction would look like. Anne kept a careful eye on the foreman, even correcting an error in the floor plan that he had completely overlooked.

Elizabeth and David Arrive on the Scene

In March 1980, I received promotion to associate professor. This meant that my future at Duke was secure, at least for the next several years. That was a huge relief, for the threat of being dropped from the list of academic faculty was now gone. Without this promotion, my fate at the institution would have indeed become precarious. Now, I could finally relax a bit more about my career!

That same year, Anne became pregnant with our first child and our lives, of course, were about to undergo a huge change. Even though I was now 38, I had no real understanding of how much life would be altered, perhaps because I was an only child and a very spoilt one at that. At any rate, I was really an inconsiderate and selfish father. After a long and difficult labor, our first child, Elizabeth Shire Kelvin, arrived on October 13, 1981, weighing in at a sensible 6lbs 13oz. Like all babies, she was immediately declared lovely. Life was now on a new path, of course, with Anne bearing the brunt of this change.

I was, of course, extremely happy at Elizabeth's arrival, but, despite this, held back from being a helping hand. As I already mentioned, I had never assumed responsibility for any domestic duties. And now, I must admit to rarely, if ever, changing a diaper. Clearly, I showed myself to be highly immature in this new dynamic.

I wonder if my failure to remember my early childhood, coupled with the subsequent absence of any definable family life, is what made me so singularly immune to being helpful and considerate. Other than my father pottering around in his beloved greenhouse, I have no recollection of him rolling up his sleeves at home at any stage of my existence to participate in rearing me or in carrying out any housework. But, perhaps, that's a rather weak defense to bring up!

Anne, being one of three siblings, favored having three offspring herself. I, on the other hand, felt one was sufficient, especially if we wanted to give our children, in true Jewish style, the best of everything. So, we compromised, and settled for two. Parenthetically, we would now have four for doubles in tennis as well as a foursome for golf.

Our second child, David Alexander Kelvin, arrived on June 7, 1983, and this time Anne's labor was a relatively rapid affair. He was heavier than Elizabeth, weighing a solid 8lbs 6oz. It would be fair to characterize him as a chubby baby. As usually happens after a few years, though, his baby fat receded. Anne, now surrounded by two babies, resigned from her position as a physician's assistant and, her hands being full, did not return to the work force until David was seven years old.

Back Home in Leeds, in a Professional Capacity

Meanwhile, I had become friendly with Hans Herlinger, who I met at the Society of Super Great Radiologists. We had in common that he lived in Leeds and we often played golf together at the SGR annual meetings. Hans was an Austrian Jew and had lost his father and many family members in the Holocaust. He later wrote a spellbinding memoir that documented his escape from Austria, and his time in Malta, Uganda, and British Guiana before finally reaching Leeds where he became a highly respected radiologist.

It was in Leeds that he was instrumental in organizing an annual multidisciplinary course in gastrointestinal radiology to which I was invited in 1982 as a North American guest speaker. Subsequently, I was asked back to my hometown on several occasions to participate in these courses. These were unexpected bonuses to my career, for they enabled me to see my father and Donnie each time I returned, as well as to reconnect with childhood friends. It struck me that, while many of these childhood friends had travelled widely since growing up there, they were still unable (or unwilling) to break away from the stranglehold of the Leeds Jewish community.

Sabbatical at the Mayo Clinic

After seven years at Duke, I was eligible for a six-month sabbatical. Most physicians took advantage of this opportunity to travel to a relatively exotic location, but with two babies this seemed a stretch and likely a logistic nightmare. Accordingly, I made arrangements to take my sabbatical in 1984 at the Mayo Clinic in Rochester, Minnesota, taking care to ensure that I was there from April to October since winters there are brutally cold. I had been a visiting professor at the Mayo Clinic two years previously, so I was well acquainted with its excellence. At that time, I was so nervous at the thought of speaking at such a renowned institution that I was unable to sleep a wink the night beforehand. A dinner was held the evening after my talk, and I remember nodding off more than once out of sheer exhaustion.

My task at the Mayo Clinic was to beef up my skills in computed tomography (CT). The Mayo Clinic was an extraordinary experience. My first impression was that everyone behaved in a very gentlemanly fashion. I only once heard a physician raise his or her voice during the six months that I was there, and he was an irascible Irishman. The level of clinical care and knowledge was exemplary. The well-known maxim that someone with a rare disorder should visit the Mayo Clinic for treatment was entirely correct. If other teaching institutions had only seen 20 or so cases of a highly unusual disorder, the Mayo Clinic would almost certainly have seen more than ten times as many.

The standard of care for straightforward disorders was also extremely high. I underwent a minor surgical procedure there to ensure that our family would not undergo any further increase in size and the care that I received was outstanding. The clinic had no time for big egos or star-struck physicians; clinical practice was clearly a team effort with no one allowed to get out of control. Unlike at Duke, there were essentially no prima donnas.

The winters there were rigorous, but many who worked at the clinic were of sturdy Scandinavian stock and could handle these harsh conditions with impunity. For those who eventually found the winters too daunting, there were now opportunities to go south to Mayo's new campuses in Scottsdale, Arizona, and Jacksonville, Florida. Since then, additional facilities have been opened in both Abu Dhabi and London. The Mayo Clinic is now considered the leading medical facility in the world. While I was there, there was a modesty and humility in how physicians functioned which other medical institutions would do well to adopt.

During my sabbatical at the Mayo Clinic, Anne had a really trying time with our two children, especially as I failed to provide more than a smattering of help. I really regret missing out on so much of the experience of watching and helping them evolve during this very early part of their lives. It was very unfair to burden Anne with so much of the responsibility, and I now realize how disappointing this must have been for her.

The Book No One Read

Around this time, Richard Gardiner, a friend from the SGR, had assembled a number of radiologists to compile a large book on gastrointestinal radiology. I was assigned the task of writing the chapter on the large bowel. There was only one problem that Richard had to face: many of the contributing radiologists were far better known and busier with academic pursuits than he. Accordingly, many deadlines for his magnum opus came and went, despite his repeated pleas for them to complete their tasks. He was in over his head and had violated a basic principle: do not ask those better known than yourself to come forward and expect them to pitch in. As it turned out, only myself and one other radiologist who had "committed" to the book completed their chapters. I frequently called Richard about this delay, and he would complain about dereliction of duty, while at the same time subjecting me to tedious and lengthy accounts of his newly found love…for a woman that I had never met.

It became increasingly clear that his goal was unattainable. I then proceeded to make one of the most foolish decisions of my life. Having the opportunity to expand my chapter into a stand-alone book, I decided to run with the idea. My real folly was that I took this decision as an invitation to significantly expand and upgrade its content and so I spent the next two or so years heavily committed to this task. This, of course, coincided with the early childhood days of Elizabeth and David and so I became even less useful to Anne in helping her and spending time with them. This was clearly a classic case of satisfying my ego at the expense of others. To add insult to injury (although the book was well reviewed), by the time it was published in 1987, endoscopy had already made significant inroads into the radiologists' world of barium. Accordingly, very few copies were sold.

New Job, New City

As our time at the Mayo Clinic was drawing to an end, Dean Maglinte, a friend that I knew from the SGR, told me about an opportunity to move to Methodist Hospital in Indianapolis. The hospital was opening a large outpatient center and needed a second radiologist devoted to barium studies of the gastro-intestinal tract. The opportunity was appealing not only because of the marked increase in pay associated with working in the private sector, but also because of the continuing opportunity to both teach and write papers, for Methodist had its own residency programs and Dean was a noted and original contributor to the radiologic journals. His interest was primarily the small bowel, whereas mine was the large bowel. Anne and I agreed that I should pursue this opportunity. So it was that, on our way back to North Carolina, we stopped in Indianapolis.

I was shown around Methodist Hospital and where the new outpatient center would be built. Everyone was very friendly. I was taken for dinner to St. Elmo's Restaurant, not realizing that this was a famed institution in downtown Indianapolis. We sat at a long table near the bar. It was noisy, to say the least. I had their famous shrimp cocktail, the fiery sauce of which nearly burnt a hole in my esophagus. This visit nevertheless convinced me that a move to Indianapolis with the opportunity to work at an outstanding private hospital was a good idea.

There were pangs of associated guilt, since most folks returning from a sabbatical do not tell their chairman that they are about to leave. Furthermore, Duke had always looked down on private practice as corrupt and money grabbing and this disdain had been inoculated into me time after time. When people asked me where I was going, I would reply, "Methodist Hospital in Indianapolis," but hastened to add that I would continue to teach and write papers. I could not bring myself to merely say that I was going into private practice. Academia put itself on an unnaturally high pedestal, and we were all expected to follow suit.

The last few months at Duke were bittersweet, for we had made many good friends while there and being on the faculty of a rapidly developing department was stimulating, even if this was associated with considerable pressure to perform. We knew we would miss both Jeff and Rose, and Reed and Martha Rice, among many others. I had slowly grown to feel more comfortable at Duke than at any other location to date, probably because I was not constrained by any societal impositions. The only constraint there was the need to stay focused on one's career.

Part Five

MIDDLE YEARS: INDIANAPOLIS

Move to Indianapolis

At the end of June 1985, Anne, Elizabeth, David and I (our children were now almost 4 and 2 years old respectively) moved to Indianapolis. We chose to live in Zionsville, a charming small town northwest of the city, because it had an excellent school system and because Anne's brother John was already living two streets away from the house that we bought in Colony Woods. Anne's other brother, Bob, had not yet moved to Indianapolis from Cleveland.

Zionsville was a quaint town that boasted quirky shops on its brick-lined main street which attracted a considerable number of tourists. Its population was almost entirely white. Even now, 35 years later, ninety percent of the inhabitants are white, while African Americans still only account for less than two percent and Asians less than five percent of the population. Christianity was clearly the dominant force in the community. While we were living there, there may have been ten Jewish families, at most.

Our new neighborhood was a fun one. As the children grew older, they would spill into each other's yards and the parents accepted this without any problem. Almost none of the homes were fenced off. It was all very relaxed and open, and our house bordered a pond. One day, David fell into the water and for a moment or two I panicked that he might drown. Fortunately, we fished him out quickly and all was well. From the get-go, Elizabeth was self-assured whereas David was clearly uncomfortable handling preschool. This showed in his reluctance to join in the circle of children. He would hover unhappily outside the perimeter of the group. In years to come, this early shyness was replaced by a far more confident and comfortable persona.

It was good to get away from the intense heat and humidity of North Carolina's summers, although temperatures in Indianapolis would sometimes approach those we had previously experienced. Through Anne's brother John and his wife Barb, we made some friends. Elizabeth and David quickly established friendships in the immediate neighborhood. Once they started in elementary school, their circle of friends increased through the auspices of respective parents.

I took up golf with renewed enthusiasm, and after two years playing on a public course we joined Broadmoor Country Club, the members of which were at that time predominantly Jewish. Even so, we never identified strongly with its Jewish membership. On Friday evenings, as we introduced our children to golf, we often had the course to ourselves while many members were gathered for a traditional meal and brief service to usher in the Sabbath. As a result, we and our pull golf carts had the run of the place. We also joined Azionaqua, which had a large swimming pool that was very popular with those in the surrounding neighborhoods. When we had time, Anne and I continued to play tennis, and continued to be very evenly matched. I still had an erratic, but fast, serve and Anne continued to have the much better all-court game.

Zionsville was a huge contrast to Duke and its surrounds in the Research Triangle. There, it seemed everyone in our immediate vicinity sported an MD or PhD. While this was very stimulating, it was heavy on intellect and hardly a cross section of the real world. But then, was Zionsville representative of the real world? I had moved from very academic soil to soil that was far more down to earth but carried its own set of limitations. Here, there was homogeneity and little room for diversity and differing opinions. As one person cruelly expressed themself online: "People of Zionsville are very close minded. Everyone has to be like everyone else and fit inside their perfect box. Otherwise, you are not welcomed." I think that is greatly overstating the case, for we were always made to feel welcome. It was definitely a comfortable place in which to raise our children.

Methodist: My New Professional Home

The radiology department at Methodist Hospital certainly had its idiosyncrasies. There were many individuals who had issues with their colleagues. These issues could be expressed in a very open fashion, as each member of the department tried to establish their own territory in a rather anarchic manner. Such clashes were particularly prevalent within the abdominal section, to which I, of course, belonged. This was very different from the department at Duke, where we all had a common bond: deference to the chairman. I found these interpersonal feuds to be childish and very unappealing.

The level of clinical practice at Methodist Hospital surprised me. It considerably surpassed that of Duke, which prided itself on being one of the most celebrated hospitals in the nation. The reason was not hard to discern, for much of the faculty's efforts at Duke were directed to research. The overwhelming number of residents and fellows there spared the faculty from having to see too many patients. No wonder, then, that their clinical skills tended to have lost their edge!

Another difference was the pace at which one worked in private practice. It was far faster than at Duke, and it took a year or more for me to become acclimatized to this. When one of my partners mentioned that "productivity" was important, I was initially puzzled by what this meant. I soon learned that this referred to the speed of work required to generate the expected amount of income. After a while, I got the message, for what choice did I have?

Our best surgical residents came from Indiana University, and I could not help wondering why they did not stay in that bastion of academia. They explained that they operated on four to five times the number of cases at Methodist Hospital and were treated as human beings rather an inferior species that could be pushed around (and sometimes eliminated from the program). This was an eye opener, for I had been brainwashed into believing that the world of private practice fell far short of the lofty ideals of institutions like Duke.

I enjoyed the freedom of working at Methodist Hospital. Your fate did not lie, as I already mentioned, in the hands of a single person, your chairman. Also, I must confess to liking the salary I earned at the institution, for it was double what I was making at Duke and would be sufficient to allow our children to eventually attend any university of their choice. That was, in fact, far and away the main reason behind my move.

Opportunities to publish or give talks did not change. I was no longer under any academic pressure, but nevertheless I continued my efforts in these directions, for they allowed me to spread my wings, and meet interesting, like-minded souls. The seemingly unending number of X-rays that you were required to read was never a compelling experience for me. I needed to interact with other people to relieve the monotony. These interactions, whether inside or outside the institution, mattered, for they kept me engaged and excited. Once an extrovert, always an extrovert, I suppose.

Elementary Years with the Kids

While David was only two or three years old, we were amused to hear that he had persistent difficulty calling Elizabeth by her real name, so instead he substituted "Zee Zee." This name stuck and, to this day, I love to call her "Zee." We often visited Anne's parents, Bill and Sally Getty, in Evansville, Indiana, where the children always had a marvelous time. Once the children had reached the age of five or so, we made annual trips to Tenerife in the Canary Islands to give them the opportunity to spend time with my father and Donnie. For some reason, Donnie kept telling David that they would get married and go to Israel. I am not sure that this suggestion sat well with Elizabeth, who must have felt rather left out. These trips certainly made our children aware that there was another world, and that this world lay far beyond the confines of Zionsville.

When our children started in elementary school, it became clear that they were quick learners and so they were placed in a group that progressed in a more accelerated fashion. This more advanced placement, to a large extent, determined who were their school friends. Elizabeth became very friendly with Emily Pearce and Sara Brummett. David's best friend was Guy Curry, who lived in our neighborhood and often fetched up at our house. He seemed rather abandoned by his parents, each very caught up in their own careers. Later, David became a good friend of Brian Lawson, a bright young man with a philosophical bent that I found quite intriguing.

When the children were six or so, we took them skiing to some easy slopes in Cannonsburg, Southern Michigan. By the second day, it was clear that their abilities exceeded any challenges offered by those low mountains, so we migrated further north to Crystal Mountain where the terrain was more demanding. It was not long before we started going to Colorado for a real ski experience. There we would stay in Frisco, where we could take advantage of three mountains on one ticket: Copper, Keystone, and Breckenridge. The latter had the most available slopes, but they were set on different mountains, and it was a real pain to cross from one to the next.

One day, Elizabeth forgot to apply sunscreen which was not a good idea when skiing in strong sunlight at 10,000 or 11,000 feet. She developed terrible facial edema, which was very painful. The emergency room physician informed us that this was a second-degree sunburn. I do not remember what treatment she received but it was several days before her normal features were restored. Fortunately, there was no subsequent facial scarring.

The children started to play soccer at the age of six or so, and I was one of the coaches. The children would swarm like bees in a hive, oblivious to any position they were supposed to occupy. It was quite amusing to watch their antics. As coaches at this early stage, we had nothing to offer them. Since all English kids played soccer, though, I had fun kicking the ball around from time to time.

Once both our children had reached the age of seven, Anne started a new career: teaching all aspects of health to school children at the Ruth Lilly Health

Education Center next to Methodist Hospital. She was the only teacher with medical training. All the others were teachers adapting to the needs of the center. School children would come from all parts of Indianapolis and the surrounding areas to learn from computer-aided programs that the teachers used. It was a wonderful program, and greatly appreciated by all, but sadly is now defunct.

As a family, the four of us would often play golf together and both our children became good golfers. Starting at the age of five or six certainly helped! When David was nine, we entered the first father and son golf competition at Broadmoor, which we won. That was very exciting. On the first hole, I somehow managed to hole out from 100 yards and I think that clearly boosted our confidence.

Elizabeth was always an independent child. She knew what she wanted and went after whatever that was. David was more diffident in his early years but, as time went by, his confidence grew. For a while, when David was still chubby, Elizabeth would taunt him by calling him "fat." Not unreasonably, this upset David and sometimes he responded by hitting her. Elizabeth would then complain to us about this act of violence, carefully omitting that she had initiated this interaction. When we established that this was a "tit for tat" we were able to move on until history repeated itself.

Elizabeth and David thoroughly enjoyed our family visits to Anne's parents in Evansville. Sally and Bill loved to see them, and found all kinds of activities for them to enjoy in and around their lovely home. Our children always looked forward to these visits, for they were very pleasurable times that we all shared together.

As I have already alluded to, Anne was far more involved with the children, especially in their earliest years. Once they had reached the age of four or five, I did show more commitment, but Anne was still clearly the one who was more in charge and she monitored their behavior if they crossed any red lines (which did not happen very often). When they started playing soccer and golf, however, I appeared more on the scene. They both seemed to me to be model children, and usually showed, thanks to Anne, good manners. I was also proud that both of them were placed in the accelerated stream at school. After all, Jewish parents had always heavily stressed the importance of a good education.

Choosing a Religion for Our Children

As our children grew older, Anne and I needed to decide in what religion, if any, our children would be raised. Since my adherence to Jewish ritual was almost nonexistent and Anne was a sincere and strong Presbyterian, we decided that Elizabeth and David would be raised in the Christian faith. This seemed, at the time, a reasonable decision, although its consequences were not entirely foreseeable.

We were in the habit of celebrating Christmas, which included having a traditional Christmas tree. On Christmas Eve, we all attended a service at Anne's or my mother-in-law's church, but I drew the line at singing the carols and songs which almost always referred to Jesus. I was, however, rather fond of the melody "Silent Night." We did not completely bypass Hannukah since I usually lit the candles for its eight nights. This was my only concession to Jewish ritual during the calendar year. On several occasions, we were invited to the homes of Jewish friends to celebrate the Passover Seder. Needless to say, none of these homes were located in Zionsville.

I clearly recognize, in retrospect, that I should have provided our children with more knowledge of my background, especially since religious ritual is not a necessary component of being Jewish. In fact, most Israelis are secular and not highly committed to religious practice except at the Jewish New Year (Rosh Hashana) and the Day of Atonement (Yom Kippur). I could have introduced a minor version of one of the Seder nights at the beginning of Passover, but I realize that I would not have known how to proceed.

To allow my children to be brought up Christian without, at the same time, giving them any understanding of my Jewish roots was a mistake and, for me, a confusing situation. There is no doubt that the renouncement of my Jewish identity, coupled with frequent geographic moves, contributed to the feeling that I was a wandering "urban nomad." Nevertheless, being an outsider suited me, for I certainly did not want the leader of any group telling me what to do.

Zionsville: The Good, The Bad and The Ugly

Looking back on our 22 years in Zionsville (yes 22 years!), we were basically happy there. It felt very safe, had a small-town charm and was home to a strong school system. For most of our time there, we lived in a very open, relaxed neighborhood. Although there was considerable wealth in Zionsville, this was, on the whole, associated with a pleasing lack of ostentatiousness. There was nothing brash about the town. Indeed, a major part of its appeal was that it was relatively low key.

Nevertheless, Zionsville could lay it on when the occasion demanded. This was particularly true of the Trader's Point horse show, an annual competition that featured some of the world's best equestrians including some Olympians. Overall, there was a feeling that the town was a throwback to bygone days and most of its inhabitants felt at ease with each other as they lived a comfortable and undisturbed existence, relatively isolated from the hustle and bustle of urban life elsewhere.

Living in the past also had its downside. People often had a narrowly focused view of the outside world, from which the town seemed remarkably detached. You could argue that this was the result of growing up, generation after generation, in the middle of an essentially agricultural state. This, however, was only part of the story. I knew quite a few people who had enjoyed excellent schooling, many of whom went on to study at equally excellent universities. How then could such people remain oblivious to the changing world around them? I found this particularly disturbing because it appeared that I had exchanged my provincial Jewish background for a different provincial background, one that was the domain of satisfied Christians rather than satisfied Jews. Both worlds were, I thought, sadly out of touch.

Given the lack of diversity in an almost exclusively white, and relatively isolated, population, it should come as no surprise that racism could and would bubble to the surface, sooner or later. A white student at Zionsville High School (ZHS) invited a black friend from a neighboring school district to come and shoot hoops in the school gym. Not long thereafter, a group of ZHS kids went to the white student's home and invited him to step outside where, ostensibly, he would be the unwilling recipient of many blows. Naturally, he turned down the invitation. The next episode in this saga blew the lid clean off the top. The white student was beaten up by this group in the school playground, with two or three of the ZHS teachers witnessing this but failing to intervene.

Following this sorry state of affairs, a small organization "Zionsville United for Multicultural Appreciation" (ZUMA) was formed. There were six or seven of us on its board, of whom all but one represented a minority group, whether Black, Jewish or Hispanic. Later, a speech was given to an audience of interested individuals by a Black superintendent from the Indianapolis school district. She explained at some length that most Black people feared visiting Zionsville because they were made to feel very unwelcome if they ventured there and would receive nasty stares and glares in the shops lining its Main Street. Clearly, Black visitors were unwittingly overstepping the invisible red line meant to keep them out.

Antisemitism also lurked under the surface of this seemingly peaceful town. I once mentioned to a neighbor that I was considering joining Broadmoor Country Club. He looked at me in amazement, his jaw dropping almost to the pavement. All he could say, stammering uncomfortably, was: "But, they, they are…different." Those words "they" and "different" still haunt me to this very day. I gasped, squinting my eyes at him and gritting my teeth in utter disbelief.

So, we Jews also needed to keep our distance and stay on the other side of the fence! What on earth was I doing living here? I was blindsided. This guy had received a good education, having attended Notre Dame University, but obviously harbored long-held discriminatory beliefs. I wondered if this might be a result of a blinkered upbringing.

Later, David was attempting to grab the last spot on the ZHS golf team. Known to be half Jewish, he was subjected to antisemitic tropes, and had his ball kicked under a bridge so that he would not be able to post a competitive score. I was incensed and wanted to bring this matter up with the athletic director of ZHS. David, however, did not want to make an issue out of it, and soon made his way onto the team. In his final year, the team, on which he played a major role, would go on to win the state high school championship. While Elizabeth was in high school, a girl's golf team was established, and she also became a key player on the team.

A Daughter Who Dances, A Father who Can't

Elizabeth started ballet school in Zionsville when she was five or six. At this early age, she spent most of the time sitting on the stage in her tutu staring blankly out at the audience or other members of the young "ensemble." As time passed, her skills increased greatly and she became an accomplished dancer. I was very delinquent in watching her progress. This was partly because I was not at all enamored by the rigid formality of classical ballet, but even more so because of my complete inability to dance. Once or twice a year, we fathers joined our daughters in a father/daughter "get together." In addition to my spastic dancing, I was expected to lift and carry Elizabeth across the studio floor. Because of my skinny torso and arms, I was manifestly unable to do this. To rub this in, all the other fathers could execute this task without any problem whatsoever.

Eventually, Elizabeth was given the plum role of the Sugar Plum Fairy in the dance studio's annual performance of "The Nutcracker." This was a huge honor and made me realize just how much hard work she had put into her dance training over all the years. In a highlight moment at the end of the ballet, Elizabeth needed to descend into the strong arms of Drosselmeyer, played by one of her male dance teachers. On this occasion, it was, for a split second or two, an unsafe descent but fortunately Drosselmeyer recovered, caught Elizabeth in time, and so she escaped any injury.

Golf with Family

Golf at Broadmoor, as I mentioned, became a sport shared by all the family and we would frequently play together. At first, David would clamber up trees almost as often as he would hit the ball. I shook my head at these antics and needed to repeatedly inform him: "That is not why we are here." Elizabeth was more disciplined, perhaps because she was older. She could hit the ball a remarkably long way. We had much fun as a family. I was delighted to see them enjoy the game and watched with a smile as they gradually improved. While they later began to play with their own friends, they continued to be happy playing as a foursome with Anne and myself.

David and I bonded strongly on the course. On many an evening, after a round of golf, we would chip onto the greens for nickels and dimes until it was pitch black. Arriving home late for dinner, Anne would frown and rebuke us for our disregard of her carefully prepared food. David was keenly awaiting the day that he would finally triumph over me. I remember one occasion when he had me by the short and curlies. However, by some fluke, I holed out from a sand trap on the last hole. In his surprise at this last-minute rescue of mine, his body sagged and tears appeared. It was not long, though, before he achieved his goal and he never looked back.

Ten Years Married: A Trip to Italy

Anne and I chose to go to Italy for our tenth anniversary. We spent five days in Venice, which was magical. St. Mark's Square and the Grand Canal again exceeded all my expectations, and the absence of cars was a sheer delight. Our small hotel was near La Fenice Opera House and sometimes we could hear the singers practicing their arias. From there we went to Florence. It was horribly crowded, and noisy because of Vespas and cars, an unwelcome contrast to the quiet of Venice. Medieval paintings of floating angels did not cut it for me, and we were finished with our tour of the Uffizi Gallery in almost record time, 57 minutes to be exact. Rome was our last stop. The huge size of the city made it quite unmanageable. We booked tours with a private guide and enjoyed marvelous visits to the Forum Romanum and the Vatican in this way. Our Vatican guide appeared to be studying for the equivalent of a PhD and he treated us to some juicy scandal about popes in the early part of the twentieth century. Scandal about so-called righteous figures is right up my alleyway!

We had enjoyed our first ten years of marriage, even though I was overly caught up in my work first at Duke and then at Methodist Hospital. In both locations, we had settled comfortably into their respective backgrounds. Anne had returned to work, and very much enjoyed teaching health education at the Ruth Lilly Health Education Center. After ten years of marriage, the intense pressure of my work had finally receded. That was, after all the years of plodding along, quite a relief. We were enjoying symphony concerts and repertory theater and had developed a pleasant circle of friends. Not infrequently, we spent weekends on North Carolina's low-key coastline. Life was good.

Todd: A Family Tragedy

In 1992, a very tragic event took place. Todd, Anne's nephew and a delightful 17-year-old guy who usually drove with consummate care, was in a car accident. On this particular evening he took off in his father's BMW and roared along a country road close to our neighborhood. We received the saddest possible phone call from a physician, Tom Slama, whose home was across the road from the scene of the accident. The car had slammed into a telephone pole. Todd and his passenger friend were immediately ejected, and Todd lay, face mangled and quite dead, alongside the shattered car.

I was asked to identify his body, which looked like Todd despite the disfigurement. I had never in my life seen a sight even remotely like this. I was shaking and trembling as I confirmed that the lifeless figure was indeed Todd. I felt as if I was in an unimaginable nightmare. His passenger made it to the local hospital but died shortly after admission. Todd's sudden loss devastated the family, and undoubtedly contributed to the subsequent divorce of his parents, John and Barb. Todd's younger sisters, Anne and Alison, were teenagers who suddenly found their life turned upside down, the effects of which haunted them for many years to come. Elizabeth, aged 11, and David, aged 9, were much younger than them, but they were clearly very upset, and probably also puzzled by what had happened. Todd lived only two streets away, and he was, after all, their cousin. While they were not especially close, the children all met when a celebratory holiday on the calendar took place. I think it really affected Anne, and me too, as we were all very fond of him.

Freddie goes to Augusta!!

I clearly remember one particular day of our residents' annual graduation ceremony. During the traditional afternoon game of golf preceding the ceremony, one of the attendees, an ex-resident, stood on the 18th green, waved his arms around and loudly proclaimed: "I can get anyone on Augusta." I scratched my head and stared at him in amazement. Can you believe that I was the only golfer to take this announcement seriously? It was hard to fathom why the others would look such a gift horse in the mouth. I immediately went up to him and penciled both his phone number and email address on the scorecard. Eventually, we established a date for this "once-in-a-lifetime" experience. I was invited to give a couple of radiology talks at the Augusta University Medical Center, and my honorarium (yes, you can guess!) was to play the famed course where the Masters Tournament is played every year. What more could a golfer ask for?

I practiced my putting relentlessly before going down there. My buddies at Broadmoor had given me a very extensive shopping list, which I was still attempting to fulfill, when my host summonsed me to get ready to play the par three course before we teed off on the course proper. My handicap at the time was 13 (I had managed to break 80 twice at Broadmoor), and my goal at Augusta was to break 90. The greens were, of course, fast. One television commentator called the greens "slick as bikini wax" and the powers that be at the club, on hearing this, ensured that he was never again permitted to commentate at their famed "Masters" tournament. Although I was proud to have played the par fives in one under par, a seven at the short twelfth hole over Rae's Creek was a complete disaster. Afraid of my ball landing in the creek (as were many of the world's best players!), I over clubbed and my ball finally came to rest in the shrubbery behind the green. Nevertheless, I achieved my goal, finishing happily with an 88.

The club was very unpretentious, with lunch hardly different from that of far less hallowed country clubs, and the atmosphere was altogether low key. There were, at that time, no female members. My host, who was in his eighties and suffered from myasthenia, called all the ladies we came across in the clubhouse "Sugar" partly because it was likely a southern tradition but also because he probably could not remember their names. He was an altogether gracious gentleman and regaled me with many fascinating anecdotes of Augusta's storied past. The honorarium that I received was far and away the most satisfying one of my entire career. The whole experience at Augusta National Golf Club was a day that I will never forget!

My Father, Donnie, and Family

My father and Donnie visited us in Zionsville. It was great to see them both again on this side of the Atlantic, for our usual meeting grounds were the Canary Islands, Switzerland, or Scotland. Donnie was madly keen on shopping because items were supposedly cheaper than in the UK, so I spent a lot of time shuffling her between widely separated malls on the west and east sides of town.

We also spent time with Nada, who was my great uncle Benno's daughter-in-law. She organized for us to stay in an apartment located in Menton in the south of France, and another time in a small second home of theirs in Davos, Switzerland. Once a celebrated ski resort, the lift system there had not been updated, and the terrain was so spread out that one time we needed to take a train to return to Davos. The ski runs were poorly marked, and so we were at risk of entering potentially dangerous, unmarked territory. Nada also visited us in England and we spent enjoyable times together in Scotland.

In 1995, Anne's father Bill died unexpectedly due to a complication associated with his heart disease. I was very fond of Bill, for he was a very kind and gentle soul, as well as a truly dedicated physician. Anne's mother lived considerably longer. She developed Alzheimer's disease and needed to be in a retirement home for many of her remaining years, subsequently dying in 2014. Anne was a very devoted daughter, and made a point of frequently visiting her.

Witness for both the Prosecution and the Defense

On quite a few occasions during my career, I had the opportunity to be an expert witness in medical malpractice cases. In the belief, mistaken or not, that I had a gift for the gab, I looked forward to these opportunities. I tried to strike a balance between appearing for the defense and for the prosecution in these cases, and on several occasions turned down a case that I thought was without merit. Sometimes this led to the attorney being mightily offended. I am sure that, in such cases, the attorney often then sought an unscrupulous physician who would say anything in order to earn extra dollars. These distasteful medical whores were not uncommon.

The cases were invariably interesting, and there were frequently unexpected twists and turns. Contrary to what public opinion often asserts, I almost always found the attorneys with whom I worked to show considerable integrity. Perhaps this was because I chose carefully. At any rate, I was only once on the losing side out of the 15 or so cases that I accepted.

In that particular case, the defendant, a radiologist, had clearly missed a straightforward diagnosis of acute appendicitis on a CT study, which has an accuracy of approximately 95 percent for this disorder and is far more reliable than the physical examination. This case was the most "open and shut" one in which I was involved; a resident with only six day's experience on CT was able to make the diagnosis of appendicitis instantly. The appendix was swollen to twice its normal size and I showed this evidence to the jury, using a ruler to ensure that they clearly understood this finding. To my astonishment, the radiologist was found not guilty of medical malpractice. The trial took place in downtown Louisville, with a jury which was composed of five white and four black individuals. The defendant was a white physician, and the jury's decision was five to four along purely racial lines.

I was shocked, and discussed the case with a surgeon at Methodist Hospital who had grown up in a small Kentucky town. He informed me that any discussion of race there was taboo and suggested that I find out the race of the plaintiff. I called the attorney. "Yes," he said, "she was Black." "So," I inquired, "why did you take the case in such a racially charged town?" He replied that he did so because he saw no way that he could lose. What a striking reflection on the legal system and the state of our nation! It was one matter to encounter racism at a personal level, but quite another to see, at close quarters, that justice was similarly polluted. There are many trials, of course, where race is a huge factor in the outcome. Nevertheless, experiencing this miscarriage of justice in front of my very eyes was unassailable evidence of the chronic racism that has always affected this country.

My Father's Declining Health and its Consequences

My father's health had been declining for some time but worsened during the year 2000. I had attributed his lack of energy and appetite to depression, but this was not at all the case. He was admitted to St. James University Hospital in Leeds in the fall of that year. I immediately flew over to see him and, due to the kind and timely intervention of Tony Chapman, a radiologist that I had come to know because of my lectures in Leeds, a body CT scan was arranged for the next day. I was aghast at the results: my father had colon cancer that had metastasized to the liver and was now obstructing his small bowel. He was in a great deal of pain and required doses of morphine. It was not long before he was admitted to a hospice, where he asked the nurses to speed up the delivery of morphine which they, of course, refused to do. Though not at all religious, he kept pointing his finger upwards towards heaven with a wry, mischievous smile on his face.

My father had always been very reserved and unwilling to show emotion, except when faced with the loss of a close family member. He now was finally able to demonstrate how much he loved us. I had brought him a family photograph of Elizabeth, David, Anne and myself and he kept this by his bedside the whole time, often clutching it close to his heart. He looked at Donnie, me and John Farago (see below) with great warmth and love. He was sometimes in tears and gave gestures of almost biblical blessing (!) to all of us.

I had to return home because I was completely out of "vacation time," knowing full well that I would not see him again. Nothing could have been more heartbreaking. My father had always been my guiding light, and now I was leaving him to die after failing to recognize that his decline was not in any way caused by mental issues. The guilt surrounding these circumstances was overwhelming, but it was a cross I had to bear. Although we had been separated for many years by 3,000 miles, I had always felt much closer to him than this distance would suggest. It was as if the bottom had fallen out of my world.

I, of course, returned for my father's funeral, which was arranged by the reform synagogue to which he belonged. It was a very simple burial service, at which I said a few words about him and read the Mourner's Kaddish. Afterwards, we all went to my home in Sandhill Oval, where 30 or so of both my father's and my friends gathered informally. My father had never been one for formal ceremonies of any kind, and would not have wanted that for himself now.

My father had lived almost twice as long as my mother; her death seemed an eternity away. She should have had a much longer life and, with the advances in modern medicine, this would have been the case nowadays. He had enjoyed a wonderful childhood, and then, amazingly, found a way for him and my mother to escape from the terrors of living under the Nazis. On coming to England, they fashioned new lives for themselves. They were survivors and survived with style. By good fortune, he then came to enjoy many more very happy years with Donnie in his second marriage.

Just two months ago, in February 2022, Donnie made a special trip from London to Leeds to plant a tree that she had sponsored in my father's name for a refugee organization at a nearby synagogue. I was very touched that she had done this in honor of my father, who she deeply loved.

John Farago: a Very Kind Relation who Married Donnie

Donnie and I were at a loss as to how to handle what needed to be done after my father had passed away, but a relation of mine, John Farago, who was a second cousin on my father's side, provided enormous help in handling the many issues that we faced.

Donnie had, for some time, been going sporadically to London to take courses in alternative healing techniques, as well as treating clients there. When she did so, she had often stayed at John's home in Wimbledon directly across from the famed All England Tennis Club, where the Wimbledon Tennis Championship was played each year. Over the years, I had come to know John very well, and was extremely fond of him. While my father was alive, he had twice urged Donnie to marry him, knowing that he would take good care of her. A year or so after my father died, John indeed proposed, and they were married. I was very happy for both of them.

After living in Wimbledon for some time, Donnie and John moved into a smaller house in Deal, a charming old town on England's south coast. On the occasion of John's 80th birthday, Anne and I visited them for a lovely celebratory party. After this, we all travelled to Vienna, where John was able to locate both my parent's elegant apartment building and the family's shoe factory.

My father had tried unsuccessfully to obtain compensation for these stolen properties that the Nazis had appropriated for themselves. The Austrian government mounted obstacle after obstacle, and I was unwilling to pursue this further, for attempts at restitution were clearly going nowhere.

We also went to Sopron, just across the border in Hungary, a beautiful old town where John had close relations. Our final destination was Prague, a city that was completely preserved, and a joy to visit. There, we were fascinated by its castle, the nearby St. Vitus Cathedral, and the large, rambling Jewish Quarter. We also fitted in a splendid performance of "The Barber of Seville" at the very ornate Prague Opera House.

John's escape from Austria in early 1939 was by an entirely different route than that taken by others in my immediate family. His parents, realizing that they might not be able to escape, managed to send him by unaccompanied

Kindertransport to Belgium. Kindertransport (children's transport) was a rescue operation authorized by the British government following Kristallnacht. As a result of this operation, 10,000 children, mainly Jewish, were saved from Nazi brutality. John's parents were later able to obtain permission to come to England just a few weeks before the onset of World War II. They became butler and cook to a family living near London, and eventually John was able to rejoin them.

Snorin'

Snoring had been a nightly occurrence for some time, and Anne thought that I should be tested for sleep apnea, an idea I continually pooh-poohed. However, while driving home one afternoon, I fell asleep at the wheel and crossed the median before awakening. It did seem time, I thought, to check out why I was snoring. The test for sleep apnea involved an overnight stay in a room in which different parts of your body were hooked up to equipment in order to monitor heart, lung, and brain activity as well as blood oxygen levels. Despite all this paraphernalia, you were expected to sleep! The test was highly positive for sleep apnea. Shortly thereafter, I was fitted with a CPAP (continuous positive air pressure) mask that would keep my otherwise obstructed upper airway open. While being fitted and needing to listen to the instructions, I, not surprisingly, fell fast asleep. However, once I started using the CPAP mask, I woke up refreshed and experienced extreme euphoria for several weeks as if I was on a drug high. It is a pity that phase did not last longer!

Relaxing with Family (Old and New) and Friends

When major holidays rolled around, our immediate family always gathered together to celebrate the occasion. Anne's brothers, John and Bob, would congregate with us and enjoy a feast of food and each other's good company. Anne and John took the lead in organizing these get-togethers, especially when it came to food preparation. Bob pretended that he was being dragged to join in, but it was nevertheless obvious that he, too, enjoyed these times together.

Anne and me, Zionsville

David and me

Dad,

Thanks for being a great dad. Thanks for taking the time to play golf with me, demanding nothing more than I have fun, and teaching me that the way I deal with bad shots or bad rounds defines me. I am grateful that you taught me these lessons. I am lucky to have you as my dad.

I will treasure our golfing memories forever. And I will always find time to play a round of golf with you when I come home. I love you.

- David

David talks about golf

Elizabeth is ready to dance

Anne watches happily

Donnie is married to John Farago, my second cousin

Thanksgiving and Christmas were, obviously, the most celebratory occasions. We had a Christmas tree, at first a rather tall real one that often teetered while being assigned its spot in the living room. Later, we substituted an artificial tree that was far easier to put in place. On Christmas day, the whole family gathered and had much fun opening presents as well as eating handsomely. John was a particularly good cook and took great pride in preparing delicious meat dishes as well as tasty appetizers.

In January 2011 (yes, I'm jumping ahead, I know) John married Faith Rouch in a small, dignified ceremony at Second Presbyterian Church in Indianapolis. Faith was a delight: vivacious, caring, smart and much more. It was wonderful to have her now in our family. Her children Josh, Andrea and Stephanie were all great characters, each in very different ways!

Anne and I played social mixed doubles tennis on a regular basis for a while. Anne had become a strong doubles player, and recognized the importance of being at the net whereas I often played from the baseline and was content to lob ad infinitum. Many a time, Anne would urge me to venture up to the net but I was reluctant to do so. We frequently played bridge with three other couples: the Pearces, the Jones and the Hutchinsons. We became good friends with Jim and Amy Pearce, and Anne's best friend became Lisa Jones. Tragically, Amy died in midlife after a long battle with oral cancer.

We went skiing in Aspen several times, each time staying in a luxurious mountain home that we rented on Snowmass Mountain with ski-in/ski-out being a real perk. This was arranged by Bill Johnson, a charismatic guy who had made a small fortune with Parametric, a rapidly surging technology company. With his wife Karen, and Mike and Joanne Hayden, we had wonderful times together. I loved Snowmass, with its multitude of intermediate slopes. Black was overkill (no pun intended), and green was akin to a flat pancake, but the blue runs suited me just fine.

Feminism reaches the Pelvic Floor

My work was becoming less satisfying because of the inroads being made by endoscopy into examining the gastrointestinal system. To maintain my usefulness (i.e., to continue generating income), I was asked to read body CT scans and, like everyone else, a pile of chest X-rays. As so often happens, it was necessary to adapt to the rapid changes in the medical world and I became increasingly disenchanted with my changed role in the department.

Fortunately, a knight in shining armor came to my rescue in the form of a pioneering surgeon, Dr. Tom Benson. Tom was a moving force in the new specialty of urogynecology, which combined not only the two fields of urology and gynecology, but also that of proctology (you know...those disorders of the rectum). This holistic approach to disorders of the female pelvic floor, more commonly known as prolapse, was nothing short of revolutionary. It was a novel twist to traditional practice in which the urologist, gynecologist, and colorectal surgeon all jealously guarded their patients' various organs.

The lack of research, and an integrated approach to the management of prolapse, was undoubtedly in part a result of disinterest by male medical practitioners who full well knew these disorders were essentially limited to the opposite gender. I witnessed firsthand the frustration and anger of female practitioners who were now enthusiastically pioneering this new approach to diagnosis and treatment. Tom Benson joined forces with Dr. Linda Brubaker at Rush University Medical College in Chicago to play key roles in leading this charge.

Encouraged by Tom's enthusiasm, I became interested in the radiology of prolapse and this radically transformed the last 15 years of my career. Dean Maglinte, an internationally recognized authority on radiology of the small bowel, continued to be devoted to improving methods of evaluating this part of the gut and asked me to take the lead in developing a radiologic technique for evaluating prolapse.

The technique was a complicated one, and I will spare you all the details of what was involved. It was necessary to have the patient actually evacuate their rectal contents. This was accomplished by the patient sitting on a specially built commode, but only after the bladder and vagina were first filled with radio-opaque contrast material. These multiple intrusions were obviously highly embarrassing for the patient. To reduce their anxiety, I usually came up with one or two throw-away lines, such as when I asked the patient to "squeeze their bottom muscles tight" I would add, "Imagine you're trying to hold onto a thousand dollar note." I think this cheesy sort of humor relaxed the patient and was appreciated. One colorectal surgeon told me: "You're the only radiologist I want for this study. Nobody else can take patients through this ordeal and have them come away laughing."

Our group at Methodist Hospital, which came to include Dr. Douglass Hale, a Fellow who joined the urogynecology staff, went on to expand interest in this rapidly developing field. Dr. Benson had made us radiologic pioneers in the technique, which we called "dynamic cystoproctography." Many publications followed, and I gave talks on the subject in a wide variety of locations, including San Francisco, Chicago, Leeds, London, and Amsterdam. We published quite a few scientific and review articles, as well as several book chapters related to the subject, between 1992 and 2004. By that time, I had nothing new to say and therefore declined further invitations to present or publish what would have been merely repetitious information.

Elizabeth Evangelizes

During their teenage years, both our children were exposed to "lockdowns" during which the main purpose was to increase their belief in Christianity. Several parents came and talked movingly about what Christianity meant to them and how it helped them in their journey through life. This was followed, on the second day, by a very large influx of parents gathering in the church presumably to reinforce this message. David was not impressed and thought it all rather cultish. He was, though, in the distinct minority and so kept his thoughts to himself. Elizabeth, on the other hand, was clearly moved by the messages and became a much stronger believer. I found this alarming for, while I had agreed to their Christian upbringing, I never anticipated that either of them would fall hook, line, and sinker into extreme devotion to the church.

At some point, Anne and I were airbound for an SGR meeting in Kauai. Elizabeth had given me the gift of a beautifully wrapped book, with instructions not to open it until we were in the clouds. I imagined the book would contain tips on how to improve my confidence in putting (I had begun to suffer from the putting "yips," a deadly disease in which you freeze over the ball for untold seconds). So, once we were in the clouds, I opened her present with high hopes of receiving some well-intentioned golfing advice. The book, to my dismay, did not address my problems with putting, or other aspects of the game. Instead, I saw that the cover of the book carried the title, "Jesus, the Carpenter." Obviously, Elizabeth's expectation was that I would read it and thereby come to see the light. I spent some time pondering how to handle this situation, and finally came up with a solution. I would select a carefully researched book about all the world's religions. If Elizabeth read it, I would in turn read her book about Jesus.

She accepted this quid pro quo, and duly received the book that I chose. She did not read it perhaps because, like so many other religious people, Christians have made the assumption that they have "got it right" whereas all others must clearly be in the wrong. This "we vs. them" approach, as we know all too well, had dire consequences for centuries. After Elizabeth went to college, she closely befriended quite a few Jewish students, and her messianic fervor correspondingly diminished. I then breathed a sigh of relief while, at the same time, realizing that Judaism was not without its own set of flaws.

ELIZABETH AND DAVID: THE HIGH SCHOOL YEARS, AND "WHERE AFTERWARDS?"

Elizabeth and David continued to be stalwart students academically, and both found time to play plenty of golf on their high school teams. David was valedictorian of his class, a richlyl-deserved achievement, and Elizabeth, in a much tougher class, was one of the top eight or nine students. Elizabeth's intent was to eventually go to law school. Many of my cousins in the northeast were attorneys, and/or had married attorneys, so this career avenue was very much in my family's blood on my mother's side. Elizabeth was very disciplined and took her work seriously.

Elizabeth had sessions with a private college counsellor, who grossly underestimated her academic potential. Finally, though, she stumbled across Washington University in St. Louis, Missouri, to which she applied and was accepted. Her intent was to major in political science, prior to law school, and to minor in dance. However, once the dance faculty realized that she had no intention of pursuing dance professionally, the faculty and Elizabeth pirouetted out of each other's ways.

David sought a college with a strong engineering program, but also one that would offer an opportunity to walk onto the college golf team. He would have been accepted at Cornell University, both academically and on the golf team, but declined this opportunity because the golf season was only six weeks long in those northern climes. He eventually chose Rice University, where, in 2002, he immediately walked onto the team.

ELIZABETH AND DAVID HEAD OFF TO COLLEGE

When Elizabeth started at Washington University in 2000, I had carefully composed a speech about her embarking on a voyage of exploration and excitement. However, I broke down in tears toward the end of this message. For

David, on the other hand, I just waved goodbye. Such is the difference between father and daughter, and father and son.

Elizabeth and David both had great experiences in college, though chemical engineering was, according to David, very taxing. He wanted to quit and, instead, go to medical school. I told him to stay the course, for, if he could handle engineering, he could take on virtually any career that subsequently came his way. Unfortunately, he had to step down from the golf team roster after a year and a half, as the pressure of studying chemical engineering and showing up almost daily for golf practice was proving far too daunting. Until this time, he had acquitted(?) himself honorably on the team in several matches.

Elizabeth seemed very comfortable studying political science and she developed a side interest in international relations. She took advantage of the latter by spending one semester in Madrid, Spain. We visited her there, where she was obviously becoming more fluent in Spanish as well as enjoying the experience of a thoroughly different culture. In her second year, she shared an apartment with others, some of whom were Jewish and came from wealthy backgrounds. Consequently, any previous efforts of ours to maintain a frugal and non-materialistic approach to life immediately went down the drain.

David had started at Rice University in 2002. It had a very diverse student body, and a wonderful residential college system. In addition, the campus was a beautiful one, and the tuition was ridiculously low for a school with such a strong reputation. Twenty five percent of his class were fellow valedictorians, and he claimed to feel less comfortable than many of his peers in chemical engineering. He persevered, however, and was clearly underestimating his skills for the head of chemical engineering told Anne and me that he was one of the better pupils in his class.

He thoroughly enjoyed the residential college system and made many good friends during his time at Rice. While in college, he took time off to spend two separate periods with "Engineers without Borders" in El Salvador, where he and his team helped build a clean water system for an impoverished village. He also went to a remote, hilly part of Peru with a different organization to help start the construction of a bridge that would connect two isolated villages. During that time, he had the opportunity to witness a local religious festival with a Peruvian construction worker on the team. He had become very friendly with him and his family. David left the celebration early, only to later find out that his friend had been murdered in the afternoon toward the end of the festival's activities. He was, not surprisingly, stunned by this and wanted to return to the worker's village to better understand what had transpired. We speculated that an intoxicated local might have been settling an old score, and told him to stay away from the village but, by all means, send condolences and money to the victim's family.

My overall impression is that both of our children gained much from being in a more diverse setting than back home in Indiana and, as both were adventurous in different ways, I knew it was unlikely that they would ever return. I was not sure that Anne fully agreed with this approach, but I firmly believed it to be in our children's best interests. I suppose we were both very much colored by our own very different backgrounds.

Empty Nesting, Now and Later

Once our children were in college, we obviously had more time for our own pursuits. This was especially true for Anne, who had played the main role in the children's upbringing. Anne had many outlets in which she participated. She had always been an avid piano player, despite realizing that Carnegie Hall was still not yet in the cards. She also was a very involved volunteer for the food pantry that was organized by her church, the Zionsville Presbyterian Church (ZPC). In later years, after retirement, Anne worked at a local hospice, provided dog therapy with her best friend Lisa for inpatients at the nearby IU Health North Hospital, and attended bible study class at ZPC on a regular basis.

Unlike me, Anne was dedicated to helping, in many ways, the local community. This did not mean that there was no time to play serious, as well as social, tennis, for Anne played a prominent role on one of the teams at the Carmel Racquet Club. The two of us also enjoyed playing golf together at Broadmoor. We were part of a group in the neighborhood that played social bridge. I was pathetically inept at the game, but enjoyed chatting, distracting the more committed players, and eating far more than my fair share of available food.

Both of us regularly attended plays performed at the Indiana Repertory Theater, and concerts given by the Indianapolis Symphony Orchestra. If the music was too difficult for me to understand, I would resort to reading the excellent program notes and learned about the foibles of both famous and lesser-known composers. Gossip about great people always fascinated me!

Since I was still working at Methodist Hospital and continued to write and give talks about the female pelvic floor, I had less available time on my hands than Anne. Nevertheless, Anne continued to teach at the Ruth Lilly Health Education Center. Her life remained very busy and, quite frankly, I still do not understand how she was able to handle it all. I played a lot of golf, and regularly enjoyed the symphony and theater, but my life was relatively one dimensional compared to hers.

Our Last Lengthy Family Vacation

Anne and I knew that opportunities to take both our children on an extended family trip might be shrinking, so we all took a cruise to the Caribbean in December 2005. It was a huge ship, with lots of activities including a casino that transfixed Elizabeth and David more and more as the evenings wore on. We visited the Dominican Republic, Grenada, St. Kitts, Barbados, St. Johns and St. Thomas.

On our first evening, we attended a very colorful show in the Dominican Republic. The performers, both male and female, were strikingly handsome, and the female artists were surprisingly tall. After the show, the performers picked out several members of the audience to come up and dance. A stunning female performer, without much in the way of clothing, grabbed me. I attempted, hopelessly, to dance alongside her, doing my very best not to stare at her mammary glands which were facing me at eye level. When I rejoined the family, Elizabeth admonished me: "Dad, when you dance, you are supposed to move your lower body and not just wave your arms." And so, I learned what had been holding me back all these years.

Grenada was very lush and beautiful. I found Barbados to be distinctly uninteresting, seeing only sandy beaches bordered by huge, walled-off homes. On St. Thomas, we escaped the tourist-laden main town, Charlotte Amalie, and took a taxi to the other side of the island where a lovely, uncrowded beach named Sapphire Bay awaited us. We snorkeled in its brilliantly clear waters and, somehow, I managed to break off part of a tooth while so engaged. St. Kitts was low key and lovely, and we enjoyed a leisurely time on one of its delightful beaches.

Moe, Dog of Dogs

Anne was far more of a dog person than I. While I enjoyed having them around, it was Anne who always fed and walked them. While I loved dogs in my own way, I was never much involved in caring for them. Previously, we had a golden retriever named Julie, who was both handsome and very faithful. In February 2006, Anne's (and my) second dog, the much-loved Labrador retriever Moe, had to be put to sleep. This was a very sad moment, especially as Moe had been with us almost all her life. She had always been a very affectionate friend to the family.

Not long thereafter, Anne acquired a Cavalier King Charles Spaniel named Zoe who was cute looking but had a chronic fear of anyone other than Anne and was unwilling to venture far from our backdoor. I am no neurologist, but there were definitely a few screws loose in Zoe's head. Despite this, Anne adored her, and they bonded strongly. Later, when Zoe also needed to be put to sleep, it was again a painful and sad time. We now have a fourth dog, Sophie, who is a curious mix of a Cavalier King Charles Spaniel and a poodle. She is a bundle of fun and I really adore her. I am now working on making this feeling a mutual one, and it seems to be succeeding, since she frequently comes to visit me to receive much welcomed tummy rubs.

All Those Talks: Blabber, Blabber, and still more Blabber

Continuing as a member of the Society of Great Radiologists (SGR) remained a pleasure. I made many friends at these meetings. One in particular was Giles Stevenson, a delightful guy with much wisdom and good humor. When our wives did not join us for one of these meetings, we would room together and play golf, sometimes even before the day's talks had concluded.

I almost invariably gave a talk when I went to these meetings, most often on colon cancer or inflammatory bowel disease. When the bottom fell out of the large bowel, I started to talk about prolapse and the female pelvic floor. The main radiologic society in the United States, the Radiological Society of North America (RSNA) always held its annual meeting in Chicago the week before Thanksgiving. The weather, of course, could be very cold, but we thoroughly enjoyed browsing the stores on Michigan Avenue and visiting the amazing Art Institute of Chicago. One time, we took a boat tour on the Chicago River and saw the city's world-renowned architecture from an entirely different perspective. Chicago, though a very large city, had a distinctly friendly feeling. This may have been a reflection of the unassuming warmth and lack of pretension that was so characteristic of the Midwest.

In March 2005, Giles Stevenson and I were invited to give talks at the University of Alabama (UAB). One of my talks, "Alas, poor barium, I knew him well, a fellow of intimate images," was a play on Hamlet's monologue when coming across the skull of Yorick, the gravedigger. After this short stint at UAB, Giles and I played golf on several of the courses that constituted the Robert Trent Jones Trail. It was pure golf, with no resort activity of any kind. The courses were tough, but we had a marvelous time. The two talks at UAB spelled the end of the speaking engagements during my career, which had somehow reached the absurd number of 141. I suspect my British accent had played a large part in getting me on the podium that many times.

A Few Favorite Moments from My Career

The favorite of them all? That's an easy one: RETIREMENT. Don't believe me? Well, let me repeat myself: retirement… retirement…retirement. I think, by now, you've got it!

Other favorite moments took place, as I mentioned, when I was working in Southampton, England. My bosses there were very much into making us underlings feel "at home." Every Friday, after a teaching session, they would take us to the local pub for a very relaxed drink or two (or three). This was so different to training in London, where you never dared open your mouth unless first invited to do so. Talk about the pomposity of the English upper class!

I suppose jumping over the hurdle of yet another absurd examination could be classified as a favorite moment, but it was really more of a huge relief than anything else. It may sound faintly ridiculous, but I did enjoy hearing that a manuscript on some trivial topic that I had cooked up had been accepted for publication. I was quite proud of the fact that only one manuscript on which I had been the first author (out of a total of 34) had ever been turned down. There were also eight book chapters, as well as that damned foolish book.

I always enjoyed throwing in a joke when giving a talk. Very early on, I concluded that a joke was needed about every 15 minutes in order to save the audience from yawning or even falling asleep. These jokes separated me from the many speakers who took themselves so seriously, and they often constituted favorite moments of mine.

As I described, towards the end of my career, I focused my radiologic interest on the rectum and other organs in the pelvis. As a result, I gave quite a few talks that dealt with constipation. Realizing this topic was not exactly everyone's cup of tea, I felt that a joke would help put the audience more at ease. Googling this subject, I came across this quote by Josh Billings: "A good, reliable set of bowels is worth far more than any quantity of brains." I would also, from time to time, deliver this quote to physicians dealing with the nervous system, and, to my delight, it did sometimes upset them.

After discussing constipation, my spiel would often move further downwards to discuss the anal sphincter. Why, you may reasonably ask, would a radiologist discuss this part of our anatomy? There is a serious reason to do so, because an ultrasound examination yields highly critical information about this area, the study of which had been sadly neglected by physicians for many decades. A colleague of mine had sent me a greeting card, which showed R2D2 landing on a distant planet and staring at the backsides of its inhabitants. The caption on the card read: "Welcome to Uranus." I found projecting the image of this card to be very useful for breaking the ice and keeping the audience awake before engaging them in a discussion of investigating this remote area of the body. Medicine is, of course, a very serious career, and sensitive issues cannot be sidestepped out of embarrassment. I firmly believe that retaining a sense of humor was, on many occasions, what kept me sane.

Hello, Photography, my New Friend

Around this time, I attended a superb series of talks on photography by Dave Edelstein, who was the manager of Roberts, the main camera store in town. His talks were so illuminating that I decided to hear them a second time. As a result, I came to some understanding of the basic elements of photography. This exposure (pardon the pun) encouraged me to buy my first digital single lens reflex camera (DSLR), a Nikon D50, which allowed me more flexibility than afforded by my aging Olympus camera. Nevertheless, Dave emphasized that the gear was relatively unimportant. I still have his talks summarized in a notebook, on the cover of which is a famous admonition by Ernst Haas: "Leica, Schmeica. The camera doesn't make a bit of difference. All of them can record what you are seeing. But you have to SEE."

In early October 2006, I went on my first photoshoot out west. It was led by an elderly ex-geologist, Joe Lange. He had sent the registrants an unnecessarily long list of needed equipment, much of which, unbeknown to me, was already outdated. However, I did purchase a large tripod, which I duly lugged around wherever we went.

We met up in that absurd adult Disney fantasyland, Las Vegas, and then headed out to Death Valley, the epitome of desolation. There, we photographed the wide sweeps of the Mesquite Flat sand dunes, so vast that I got lost wandering around looking for promising subject material. We then hit Highway 395, a very scenic road through the eastern Sierra Mountains. From there, we branched out to Bristlecone Pine Forest at 10,000 feet, home to the world's oldest trees, many now twisted into unusual, modernistic shapes.

Joe realized that I was a novice nature photographer so, early on, he instructed me to "stick with the boss." I did exactly this and learned quite a bit as a result. We then went on to Mono Lake, a lake with its tufa towers rising high out of the water. There, I kept stumbling over my new, bulky tripod, so keeping up with the boss was a tough assignment. Our final stop was the Bodie State Historic Park ghost town, now preserved in a state of highly photogenic arrested decay. This photoshoot experience made a huge impression on me, especially as all the other participants were far more experienced. I guess that is learning by osmosis!

Elizabeth and Jesse, and David

Elizabeth graduated from Washington University in the summer of 2004. After applying to law schools, she was accepted to study law at Tulane University in New Orleans. I was a little concerned that New Orleans would be only too happy to offer her many distractions that might lure her away from her studies, but this did not seem to be the case. Elizabeth met Jesse Klaproth in October of her first year in law school, and I believe that it was love at first sight.

At some point in her first semester, she told me that law school was not as tough as I had suggested, and my heart sank for I knew this first semester was a crucial one. For the first time in her life, her grades suffered accordingly. The spring semester went better, and she finally scraped into the top 25 percent of her class, 25 percent being the cut off that large firms in Washington, D.C., and New York City used when recruiting.

In August 2005, Hurricane Katrina struck New Orleans and caused widespread destruction and devastation. Students had to be evacuated quickly. Elizabeth and Jesse were, fortunately, able to spend a semester at Emory University in Atlanta while some semblance of normality was restored, and they were then able to return to New Orleans in January 2006.

In 2006, because of her interest in international studies, she spent a semester in Hong Kong. There, hard work could be deferred until the last few weeks of the semester, and so she was able to fit in visits to Malaysia, Singapore, and parts of southern China. She graduated from Tulane Law School in May 2007 and, after an internship here in Indianapolis, she started to work at the huge law firm of Schulte Roth & Zabel in Manhattan where she was paid an obscene salary but received almost no responsibility.

On Halloween Day that year, Jesse found a novel way of proposing to

Elizabeth: he carved "Will U Marry Me" in the side of a large pumpkin. He may have left the question mark out, but the answer was never in doubt. Shortly before, he called me to ask my permission for him to marry Elizabeth. Before he could get too far, I interrupted him: "There's no need for a speech, we love you and are delighted that you want to become engaged." He was smart, very articulate, and genuinely caring. Each respected the other's intellect. I thought that they made a great match.

Around this time, they moved into an apartment in New York's Upper West Side, a very friendly neighborhood by New York standards. Elizabeth continued to work at Schulte Roth & Zabel at that ridiculously high salary. Jesse had joined a much smaller law firm in Fort Lee, New Jersey, where most of his clients were Korean. It was a language, of course, in which he had yet to become fluent.

David's dating had taken a more circuitous path than Elizabeth's. He dated a lovely pediatrician named Jill Roth for six years, and is now dating a guy named Asher Ai, who is a quiet, thoughtful medical physicist from China. Although, at the time of this writing, he may not have settled on a life partner, I strive only to see David happy in his relationships, even though I long ago realized his road would not be the same as mine. I could not be prouder of the person he is and shows himself to be through his role as a son, an uncle, a friend and a companion.

I do not understand from where David gets his abundance of energy. It's certainly not from me! As he was finishing at Rice University, Beyond Petroleum (BP) came on a recruiting mission. Long story short, he has been working for them ever since, including a long (too long) spell on an oil rig in the Gulf of Mexico. The rig was not far from where BP's Deepwater Horizon oil rig exploded and sank, resulting in an environmental disaster and the death of 11 workers. He could have been on it!

Not content with being a chemical engineer for BP in Houston, David later started investing in properties in non-affluent areas and lived in one quarter of one of these, which he subsequently furnished with flair, meticulous attention to detail and at some expense! He's always looking for more opportunities in this sphere of activity and would like them to be eco-sensitive.

A Pain in the Chest

On June 29, 2007, I had some chest pain that started at midnight. It kept me awake but was not severe so, in the morning, I went to work. The technologists in my area were shocked and told me that I did not look too good. I reassured them that it was probably just a virus and I would mention this mild pain to my internist when I saw him for my annual checkup that afternoon. Not satisfied, one of them went ahead and arranged for him to see me during his lunch break. I told him that all this fuss was unnecessary, but he ran an electrocardiogram on me all the same. He looked at the tracing, told me that I had had a heart attack, grabbed a wheelchair, and immediately transported me to the emergency room. So much for my cockeyed theory of a chest virus! Doctors clearly should stick to diagnosing others, and not themselves. I was admitted to my own hospital, Methodist Hospital, under the care of Dr. Doug Pitts, a superb cardiologist. After admission, stents were very quickly placed in my coronary arteries. Following a relatively uncomplicated recovery, I was allowed home a week later.

I thought that was the end of it. No way, Jose. Only ten days later, I saw Doug Pitts as an outpatient and he admitted me to a small outlying hospital after he found that I had developed a heart arrhythmia. While being monitored, I promptly decided to have a cardiac arrest, was quickly resuscitated, and was then immediately dispatched to Methodist Hospital for further management. My care there was complicated by a second cardiac arrest, a "ventricular storm" (a life-threatening situation with recurrent episodes of ventricular arrhythmia), cardiogenic shock and much more. I was intubated and sedated for about a week.

During that time, Anne and our children were there almost uninterruptedly since I could have popped off at any moment. I cannot imagine what was going through their minds while I lay there unconscious. When I was coming around a burly intensivist with whom I was well acquainted informed me, "Freddie, you've been through a rather rough time." Despite still being drowsy, I apparently replied: "Bullshit you've got the wrong patient." I think this may have helped Anne and the children to finally relax a bit, since I obviously had not completely lost my senses.

The physicians who, of course, were also my colleagues, were still at a loss as to how to effectively treat me with conservative measures, and so, eventually, I was prepared for urgent coronary artery surgery. Fortunately, a more experienced cardiac surgeon dropped in to see me and said that I would not make it off the operating table, so that plan was immediately scrubbed (sorry, another bad pun). To cut a long story short, I eventually survived (otherwise I would not be writing this stuff now) and was allowed home after a lengthy and truly complicated stay in the cardiac intensive care unit. My very caring cardiologist, Doug Pitts, gets a bottle of Glenmorangie before each Christmas holiday but deserves far more for keeping me on terra firma.

I was placed on disability until the end of the year, and not allowed to drive during that time. This was not a fun situation for Anne, who had enough to do without this added burden. I spent considerable time in cardiac rehabilitation, where I found I could walk quite a bit faster than the others who were in recovery. This was very encouraging. Anne was, quite rightly, emphatic that we needed to move to a house where we could live on one level, if needed. We looked at several neighborhoods. The one I liked most was in West Clay located in Carmel, Indiana. The houses there had a wide variety of building styles, and I had already visited them to photograph their distinctive architectural styles.

We found a charming house owned by an art dealer. Its living room was jampacked with pieces she wished to sell, which I found eclectic and rather delightful. We had privacy on two sides of the house, a small yard, and a lovely porch that overlooked one of the many ponds in the development. I was adamant that this was the place I wanted to live, and that we should stop looking elsewhere. Even though Anne took responsibility for 95 percent or more of the house and yard work, she acquiesced.

The Prius: Its Travels and its Travails

I resumed driving my beloved Prius in January 2008. At times I would "hyper-mile," which could infuriate drivers behind me who wanted to travel at a normal or faster-than-normal speed. On several occasions, I demonstrated my extreme skill using this technique and was able to extract 80 mpg from this little jewel of a hybrid vehicle. Then, one day, a young girl took a chance at an intersection near our house and crashed heavily into the driver's side door, I being the hapless driver. I was pinned down in my seat by this unexpected event. Anne happened to be at the same intersection when the accident took place. When she realized it was me inside the Prius, it must have been very alarming. The emergency medical technicians took me to the nearest emergency room at IU Health North, where I had a CT scan of my head. It revealed no acute injury, fortunately, but did show evidence of diffuse microvascular changes. These must have been the result of my cardiac arrests, the first of which was likely followed by a lapse of two or so minutes before I was resuscitated. I think my memory must have undergone some regression at the time of this cardiac arrest, but I was still clearly functional. The main problem that I subsequently developed was a penchant for entering the wrong white sedan in a car park. It is amazing how many people did not lock their car doors!

Briefly Back to the Grindstone

At the end of 2007, I needed to decide whether to return to work. Quite a few people suggested that, after what I had been through, this was not a wise idea. However, I wanted to continue to work until I was 65 and so I returned to the radiology department for the first half of 2008. My memory was good enough to be functional, and I felt that I could handle the requisite hours satisfactorily. Perhaps I was taking a chance, but I tried not to overtax myself and everything, it seemed, went smoothly.

Anne and I both retired at the end of June 2008. The radiology department threw a wonderful party for the occasion and Jonas Rydberg, a golfing friend who was by now the director of radiology at Methodist Hospital, made some very flattering remarks about me. There may have been a couple of grains of truth in what he said but flattery always goes a long way. That same week, David and I played a round of golf and, as we reached our home, Elizabeth, Anne and a large number of guests came into view. Elizabeth and David had arranged a surprise retirement party. I was very touched by this. It was wonderful to see so many friends and colleagues gathered in our modest backyard patio to celebrate the end of our careers. I did not know we had that many friends!

PART SIX
RETIREMENT AND REFLECTIONS

Stepping into Retirement: A New Beginning

For my part, as you know, I was glad to be retiring. My future would not be retirement, but rather "refirement!" I felt rejuvenated, not only to be alive but also because I knew what I wanted to do with the rest of my life. You already know what that was, of course, and it involved pressing a button on a gadget hanging on a strap wrapped around my neck.

What did I accomplish in my career? Obviously, I helped patient outcomes if I read the X-rays correctly even if I was not directly involved in their treatment. I think that I helped some residents who were burdened by so much knowledge that they felt compelled to spit much of it out in their reports. Most had been taught to produce a long list of diagnoses when it came to their final impression. I told them that this was nonsense. The referring doctor wants to know what you think is the diagnosis, not a long list of obscure and unlikely possibilities that needed "ruling out," sometimes at great expense to the patient.

On a more selfish level, I did enjoy giving talks and, though to a lesser degree, writing articles. Without those outlets, I would have gone nuts with the sheer routine of it all despite knowing that, in some cases, I was indeed helping the patient. After all this feeling of academic satisfaction, it was disarming to realize that most of my earlier pseudo-scientific contributions were for naught. Barium examination of the large bowel and stomach had been almost completely replaced by endoscopy, and so anything that I had written or said on these subjects had become, in effect, a dinosaur.

One other side benefit of being a physician was very enjoyable. Meeting smart-minded people, either through the Society of Great Radiologists or other radiologic organizations, was great fun even if some suffered from overinflated egos. This, however, was only a deadly disease when it affected that well-known species: the surgical super gods. For them, there was no cure.

I think Anne was also ready to retire, but this was partly because she had to take six months leave of absence to drive me around and keep an eye on me during my period of disablement. When she returned to work, her enthusiasm for her role of teaching at the Ruth Lilly Health Education Center had likely diminished and she chose to retire at the same time that I did. Not long thereafter, the center ceased to exist, a sad fate for an organization that had provided much useful information for so many schoolchildren.

Elizabeth and Jesse Get Married

Elizabeth and Jesse married in October 2008. The venue we chose was Tarrytown Estate, where Mark Twain had once lived for two years. The building was lovely and overlooked the Hudson River. The minister hired to officiate was a Roman Catholic priest. While Jesse was a lapsed Catholic, he agreed to having this priest marry them in order to please his family. When this pious gentleman was offered an alternative gig at a New York Yankees game, he informed Elizabeth and Jesse that he would no longer be able to officiate at their wedding. I guess the money and associated status were too much for him to turn down.

Elizabeth scurried around at the last minute to find a substitute, and came up with "Mitch the Minister," an amusing character who performed an essentially irreligious ceremony. Jesus, I believe, did not receive even one mention, which did not please Anne. The wedding took place as the sun was setting over the Hudson River, which made for a very spectacular background. Elizabeth was now Elizabeth Klaproth, and looked radiant (and yes, Jesse looked pretty good, too).

Elizabeth had hired a wedding planner, who arranged all the details for the lovely occasion. There were almost 200 guests. Anne and I wanted the wedding to be elegant but not over the top. It was not inexpensive, and the stock market had just undergone its unwelcome 2008 crash, but we were determined that everyone should have a marvelous time and that it would be a day that Elizabeth and Jesse would always remember. My father and Donnie, of course, came over for the wedding, as well as James Denton, my closest early childhood friend.

I prepared my speech in a rather unusual way. Although I had given many talks before, this one was far and away the most important. I did not want to stumble and was quite concerned about how to start it. So, I wrote the content on 5 x 7 cards and taped them together in an accordion-like bunch. I opened my speech with the cards folded in my hand and asked the guests what was the greatest invention ever. The printing press? The steam engine? The computer? Or whatever? And then I said: "No!" and let them know it was the 5 x 7 card while, at the same time, opening up the taped cards so that they fell vertically from my hand. The crowd laughed, and, from that point on, so did I. I knew that, if I lost my way, I could refer to the cards to get me back on track. Jesse's younger brother, Brendan, followed. His speech was a tour de force, filled with wit and good humor about his brother. It was truly a wonderful day, and I believe that the guests thoroughly enjoyed themselves in such lovely surroundings.

My Camera: A Second Passport

When I retired I was, as you know, already interested in photography. I am a visually oriented guy, which probably explains why I chose radiology back in the day. Dave Edelstein's talks on the basics of photography had really fired me up, and that far west photoshoot two years earlier was both a formative and dramatic experience. Now I could augment my visits to fascinating places by taking photographs in addition to just seeing the sights. This was a whole new dimension to explore!!

I started to take a camera with me wherever I travelled. It was exhilarating to meet people from many different backgrounds on more photoshoots out west, and to try to make better landscape and seascape images. I was now completely hooked. More importantly, photography started to expose me to many people beyond the confines of Zionsville and, later, Carmel.

Since I had always enjoyed the performing arts, I decided that I would offer my photographic services pro bono to arts organizations in Indianapolis. Whenever the opportunity arose, I would make a polite pitch of this offer. My first success was with Jan Virgin, the executive director of the only professional full-time contemporary dance company in town, Dance Kaleidoscope (DK). She responded by inviting me to a studio rehearsal and shortly afterwards I was given the opportunity by David Hochoy, the company's brilliant and much-loved artistic director, to shoot a dress rehearsal. This was the beginning of a longstanding association with DK which has continued to this day.

I joined the board of DK and came to treasure this relationship, about which I was very passionate. I had no business sense whatsoever; whenever budgets were discussed, the details flew way over my head. My main value to DK, other than my obvious enthusiasm for the company, was to send photographs of the dress rehearsal as fast as possible to the marketing director in order to promote their performances which started the following day.

Other opportunities to shoot dress rehearsals and performances followed, including for the Indianapolis Symphony Orchestra, the Indianapolis School of Ballet and the Kenyetta Dance Company, albeit for less sustained periods of time than with DK. I was, nevertheless, part of their action. One year, I was given permission to photograph a dress rehearsal of Indianapolis City Ballet's "An Evening with the Stars," which featured world-famous ballet dancers including Natalia Osipova of the Bolshoi Ballet, and Marcelo Gomes and Julie Kent of the American Ballet Theater. That was an unexpected and amazing experience.

These opportunities (other than the last!) extended my social circle into different spheres of artistic activity in the city south of the beltway and thereby enabled me to escape from the "soap bubbles" in which we lived. There was a standing joke that you needed a passport to cross from the northern "burbs" into the real world that was inhabited by so many people with black or brown skins. In my case, it was the camera that was the passport, and these experiences mattered greatly to me.

The people I mingled with, whether dancers, arts supporters, or philanthropists were very open minded, and tended to be non-materialistic. What I had in common with them was a love for both the visual and performing arts. No one cared whether you were gay or lesbian, or about the color of your skin. Women were very much respected and often had far more to say than men, for arts organizations (when compared with the National Football League) were very much their domain.

Where you lived and what car you drove were topics that almost never came up for conversation. I learned to better appreciate people for their ideas, and to ignore what possessions or fortunes they had amassed. Boasting about your accomplishments was frowned upon. We understood intuitively that almost everyone was accomplished in one way or another, and that this did not need to be underscored.

The Door Opens to Israel

In 2008, I also started photographing the varied performances that took place at the Jewish Community Center (JCC). As a result, I became friendly with Michele Boukai, who was the Israel and Overseas Director at the adjacent Jewish Federation. Knowing that I was a wayward Jew, she strongly encouraged me to visit Israel and, the more I thought about it, the more I became excited by the idea. I had only been to Israel once, and that was 40 years ago as a medical student. Then, in East Jerusalem, I had seen Jordanian soldiers crouching behind sandbags less than 200 yards away. Meanwhile, many of those memories had faded and I was starting to feel the need to return. I wanted to learn more about Israel, and to try to unravel what being a Jew meant. During the next eight years, I was to visit Israel five times and become artistically and culturally involved in several projects in the Western Galilee, which was in partnership with the Jewish Federations of several cities in our midwest, including Indianapolis. Once again, my camera had become a passport!

The first of these trips was a "mission," designed for American Jews to connect to their Jewish identities by exploring Israel's society and culture, and by meeting Israelis from different walks of life. We listened to lectures by prominent Israelis and visited very diverse locations that included the Holocaust Museum, the Western Wall, an enormous humanitarian food kitchen in Jerusalem, a bustling market in Tel Aviv and an elementary school in Sderot two miles from the border with Gaza. There, the children played soccer on a shortened field because they had only 15 seconds to reach a rocket shelter after the warning siren sounded.

On the last day of the "mission" we all gathered in a room and many recounted experiences that their family members had suffered, often during or after the Holocaust. Among those present were many doctors, lawyers and prominent businessmen. I did not expect any of them to choke up, but several broke down in tears as they related and listened to the horrific tragedies that had befallen their families. There were envelopes under our seats in which to enter a pledge to the Jewish Federation. Unquestionably, the collective emotional impact of the stories we heard served to heighten our contributions, for we all recognized how fortunate we were to be alive. The "mission" made a profound impact on me, for I now realized that I was inescapably Jewish and proud to be so. It had taken me almost 50 years to come to this conclusion.

Anne and I Visit Israel

Having heard about my experiences as a Jew becoming invigorated by visiting Israel, Anne became interested in going there. Being a devout Presbyterian, she wanted an experience that would allow her to see the Christian as well as the Jewish sites. Accordingly, again with Michele Boukai's aid, we found a company named Isram that arranged customized tours of the country. We started in the north of Israel, including Lake Galilee because of its strong association with

Christ and his disciples, and followed this by visiting Nazareth. Afterwards, we moved to Safed, a holy city for Jews because of their influx after their forced expulsion from Spain.

Next, we reached Jerusalem where we visited many of its important sites. From there, we took a day trip to Bethlehem. This was a very complicated affair, as we had to pass through many checkpoints. Once we reached Jesus' birthplace, we were exhorted, because of the large size of our group, to pay the guardian twice the usual entry fee. As we returned from the West Bank into Israel, we saw both the huge wall separating the two territories as well as the adjacent fencing. There was, not far away, a frustrated Arab worker banging his fists angrily against the fencing. It was not a sight that one could easily forget.

We moved on to Masada and the Dead Sea and finally visited Abi, Hans' son, and his wife Nili in Herzliya. Anne had not met them before. We spent some time with their children and delightful grandchildren. I visited Abi and Nili on several subsequent occasions. Abi suffered from depression and our relationship gradually deteriorated, unfortunately, to the point that it eventually became untenable. Anne then flew back home, while I stayed another week as a guest of the Jewish Federation's Partnership with the Western Galilee. There, I met a fellow photographer, Yochanan Kishon, and we arranged for some of his students to take photographs of their surroundings which would then be shown in the Jewish Community Center when they visited Indianapolis the following year. There were many issues associated with this process along the way which were far too tedious to explain, but this project was, nevertheless, finally completed.

Friendships, and Feelings, about Israel

In general, Israelis are very open about their feelings. This transparency is very refreshing and I enjoy their unapologetic straightforwardness. Within minutes of engaging in conversation, you can have a relatively serious discussion without the remarks being taken personally. Being able to interact in this way is very meaningful, and you can quickly acquire new perspectives.

To be in a country where the Jews were in control rather than the underdogs was, for me, an unusual feeling. For once, I felt free to say whatever I liked, without causing offense. The Jewish tradition enshrines debate and disagreement. Overall, arguments between Jewish people do not descend to the level that the participants take their differences personally. Disagreement as to how religious scriptures are to be interpreted is a core value among Jewish scholars. When it comes to politics, however, discussion can be very charged and, at times, may become personal.

Over the ensuing years, I was fortunate to make many good friends through our Partnership with the Western Galilee. Most of my visits there revolved around projects related to our art which, in my case (of course) was photography. Both myself and other visiting artists from the midwest were always warmly and genuinely welcomed into people's homes. At other times, we would meet joyously in a nearby restaurant. My closest friends were Yochanan Kishon, with whom several photographic collaborations ensued, and Eytan Hurwitz, an eclectic artist about whom you will hear more later.

The lady in charge of organizing our arts' experiences in the Western Galilee was Noa Epstein. Hers was a difficult job, because she had to accommodate the cultural differences between we Americans, who were "planners," and our Israeli friends, who were much more inclined to make last-minute decisions. Our Israeli counterparts did not always respect or understand our perspectives. However, these differences almost never impacted the warmth of individual relationships between us. Overall, I feel very grateful for the existence of the State of Israel which, at last, gave Jews a home, even though that home is far from safe.

Interlude: "How Joe Green Entered Canterbury Cathedral without a Ticket"

Warning: there is a fair amount of fabrication in this interlude!

Some folks think that all opera is nonsense. Let's take Guiseppe Verdi's "Il Trovatore" as an example. Yes, the plot is absurd. This is the opera where a gypsy woman throws the wrong baby onto the bonfire and this causes the adult surviving baby to be killed by his brother (per Sir Denis Forman). I don't remember anything remotely close to this taking place in real life. But, why does that matter? There are so many glorious arias to enjoy in "Il Trovatore" and there is, of course, that boisterous Anvil Chorus. Why deny yourself such opportunities, even if the story is fantastical. Art is, after all, a way to express your imagination. You may love or hate what it expresses. Either way, it is meant to evoke a reaction. That's what it's all about!

Giuseppe Verdi was, arguably, the greatest opera composer of all time. He wrote 28 operas, many of which are staple works that are performed time and time again (some would say far too many times). His most well-known works are "La Traviata," "Rigoletto," and "Il Trovatore" but there are many runners up, leaving poor Puccini many miles behind (in my opinion).

Although widely considered to be an Italian, you perhaps did not know that Verdi was actually a humble Englishman named Joe Green. Whenever Joe traveled to Europe, he just translated his name into Italian, hence he became Giuseppe Verdi. Joe was keenly adopted by Italian nationalists. After all, "Verdi" stands for Victor Emmanuel Re D'Italia, the first king of a united Italy. His artistic efforts, regrettably, were not fully recognized back in England. Upset with his native country's lack of respect for him, he stayed in Italy. Had I been Joe, I would have done the same. It helped that he particularly liked the way Italians laughed and waved their hands even when sober, for this only happened in England when folks were totally smashed.

Several years ago, Anne and I were staying with Donnie and John in Deal, not far from Canterbury Cathedral. We decided to pay it a visit. Yes, you do have to pay; it's a fat $18. We went inside. The place was really impressive. It is, after all, England's first cathedral. Certainly, you can get "over-cathedralled," a recurrent disease of mine, but I doubted that would happen here. I had, of course, my ever-faithful camera with me. After all, how often do you get the chance to go to Canterbury Cathedral?

Almost as soon as we entered, we heard voices, many voices. There was no indication that a service was taking place in the cathedral. Even though the cathedral is a long way from the English Channel, something fishy was going on here! As expected, I had my camera at the ready, and was gobbling up shots of the naves, aisles, and even the odd altar. Despite not being religious, I could not help feeling that I was in heaven. I wanted to shout out in ecstasy, but Anne rightly restrained me: "This is a place of worship, Freddie, not a soccer stadium." "Anne," I replied, "I thought it was soccer stadiums that were places of worship." Who's to say?

We moved on, and now we realized the source of the sounds. There was a very large chorus, and they were rehearsing my favorite choral work, Joe Green's sublimely dramatic "Requiem." It is so dramatic that it has often been called an opera in disguise! Somehow Joe had managed to squeeze through the building's massive doors without paying, quite a feat in itself. Now, I had a real dilemma: do I shoot or do I listen? I wanted to do both. And that is what I did. I kept clicking on my camera button while taking in this glorious music. If there really is a heaven, now I know, for sure, that I have had a peek.

Promoted to Grandfather

Elizabeth was expecting her first child on March 15, 2016, and everything had been going smoothly. A few weeks before delivery, however, she developed high blood pressure which led to pre-eclampsia. Treatment of this condition requires early delivery to prevent eclampsia, a serious condition characterized by seizures, and which can be fatal. She was treated with magnesium to prevent seizures as well as with antihypertensive agents. This was all very scary, to say the least. Her baby, Quinn, was delivered at 38 weeks, following which mother and, eventually baby, were fine. Naturally, we hastened as fast as possible to Philadelphia and were gratified to see that both mother and baby boy were doing well.

Eve, our second grandchild, was born on August 12, 2018, and, of course, we made our way there to celebrate her arrival, too. Unlike Quinn, who arrived prematurely, Eve went the full course. On arrival, she was a chubby, happy baby and has never looked back since. She became quite fearless and would copy much of what her elder brother did without any hesitation. It was so lovely to have a second grandchild, and to see Quinn being so affectionate towards her.

We were, of course, both delighted to be grandparents. Anne had been a model mother and was once again in her element. As for me, I had been quite delinquent during the earliest years of our own children's lives and was not about to let this happen again. We both wished that the grandchildren were closer to us than Philadelphia, but we made sure to visit them as often as possible. Elizabeth and Jesse, of course, adored Quinn and Eve, and Elizabeth threw all her energy into everything, and more, that the children needed. David was thrilled, too, and our grandchildren loved it when he came to visit. We were all eager to watch Quinn and Eve as they went through their baby years which, as always, happened far too quickly.

Hello, Havana

During my retirement years, at least until COVID-19 hit, I was an avid traveler, both with and without Anne, and frequently joined a like-minded group of others. In the latter situation, it was often with the Road Scholar travel group. Their focus was to provide educational travel experiences, primarily for older adults. Noted lecturers and well-informed guides provided inside information about the culture and society of the countries that we visited, and there were many opportunities to interact with the local population.

In July 2015, President Obama restored diplomatic relations with Cuba, and it became possible to visit the island to promote people-to-people contact with Cubans. Road Scholar programs were clearly the ideal way to make such interaction possible and so I joined one of their tours.

Our group stayed at the Hotel Nacional in Havana. This grand old hotel had a notorious history. In 1946, it was the location of the Havana Conference summit meeting of Mafia mob chiefs organized by Lucky Luciano and Meyer Lansky. This meeting set the course for the Mafia's operations for years to come, both in Cuba and the United States. The hotel's Hall of Fame room had massive photos of Churchill, Marlene Dietrich, Rocky Marciano (where else would he stay?) and many others who holed up there back in Havana's and the Mafia's heyday. It was quite a sight to behold. Incidentally, before he became president, John Kennedy had a secret tryst with three Cuban prostitutes arranged by the head of the Tampa Mafia, Santo Trafficante, who took care to watch the orgy but failed to film it, thereby missing a golden opportunity to blackmail the great man. How thoughtless can you get?

But it is the soul and spirit of Cubans today, despite their very difficult existence, that is so captivating. Everywhere (well, almost everywhere) musicians are playing, singers and dancers are heard and seen, and the children adore being photographed. Despite what Americans think, you can wander Havana's streets, see the once-elegant old buildings that are being restored and watch men ingeniously cobbling together all manners of transport. You are back in the 1950s. It is a vibrant throwback full of history and great passion.

Without doubt, our tour was sanitized so that we saw "the good side" of Cuba. There was a strong emphasis on meeting Cuban artists. We visited dance locations on three different occasions, saw the outstanding Museum of Fine Arts, and spent time at a community center outside "tourist" Havana which provided free creative opportunities for neighborhood children. One dance company that we visited, the Rosario Cardenas Danza Combinatoria, was quite well known and had performed internationally. They were a dynamic, aggressive modern dance company, and so were a treat to photograph from only three or so feet away.

Unfortunately, widespread antigovernment protests took place in 2021 in response to a rapidly worsening economic situation and the impact of the Covid virus on its already beleaguered population. This led to heavy militarization of the streets and massive detentions. It was sad to hear that a nation of such friendly, spirited people was suffering even more than previously.

Wedding, Elizabeth and Jesse, 2008

.Anne with her mother, Sally, and brothers, Bob and John

Doug Pitts, who saved my life 15 years ago, and me, 2020

Our delightful grandchildren, Quinn and Eve, 2021

I Exhibit my Photographs, and some People even Buy them!

I started exhibiting my photography quite by chance. Anne's minister and I met for lunch one summer day in 2008. Between bites, he showed me photographs of the trip that he had led to the Holy Land. The next time we met, I returned the favor and showed him mine of the same country (despite being nowhere near as holy). I had not retained the minister on commission, but he nevertheless commented on their beauty to the restaurant's owner. Bingo, the next thing I knew, my photographs were planted on the restaurant's walls, and an exhibition followed. I invited a wide range of friends, including their pets and even their hamsters. They (the friends) were very surprised to see evidence of my newfound pursuit, especially as I had only just retired from being a radiologist.

As so often happens, a chain reaction was set in motion. It started with an exhibition at the Jewish Community Center. This was the only time that I requested an exhibition; all the others were the result of an approach by others to display my art. The arts community in a sports-crazed town like Indianapolis is rather small, so word easily gets out if there is a new kid on the block. I was more than happy to be one of those new kids.

The big break occurred when I was asked to exhibit at Clowes Memorial Hall, the most spacious performing arts center in the city. The community manager for the Arts at Clowes clearly indicated that large pieces were required, since there were many large areas of wall space that needed to be filled. This was, at first, a shock to my naturally modest nature, but he ever so gently held my hand and helped make the transition to displaying bigger works relatively pain-free. The exhibition at Clowes was a turning point. With many large photographs installed in the foyer of the performing arts center, I gave two "walk and talk" tours to invited friends, the first of which attracted a crowd of about 70 to 80 people. The talk was meticulously prepared, for I had never spoken publicly to an audience about any of my art. Amazingly, people seemed interested!

As a result of the Clowes exhibition, I sold more than 20 pieces, including some larger ones. With the proceeds from this and many later exhibitions, I was able to buy a considerable amount of new photographic equipment, including, with the passage of time, four new cameras (one of which was a replacement for a camera that I cleverly dropped onto a concrete floor), as well as several lenses. I found myself running a small business and making a reasonable profit as a result of these exhibitions. It felt good to be able to buy all these items out of the profits from the works that I had on display!

Subsequently, I had exhibitions at the home of the Indianapolis Symphony Orchestra, and in a wide variety of local galleries and art spaces. Believe it or not, some of my works ended up being purchased by collectors or friends in several states, including New York, Massachusetts, Pennsylvania, Virginia, Texas, Wisconsin, and Colorado. I made sure to post my better pieces on Facebook and Instagram, and to maintain and replenish my website (https://freddiesfotosforever.com/) with newer works and styles of photography. Never a dull moment!

For the last several years, I have been a member of Art on Main Gallery in Carmel, Indiana, a gallery which is run by three delightful artists: Deb Slack, Kim Greene and Randall Scott-Harden. It is a real pleasure, and an honor to be one of the artists represented in this gallery, in which the quality of displayed art is of a high level.

I am sometimes asked, "Why do you go to the trouble of exhibiting your photography?" There is no simple answer to this. For sure, you must be thick-skinned and not allow yourself to be upset by those who cast aspersions on your brilliant concoctions. One compelling reason to exhibit is that it provides for wider recognition of your efforts. It is validating that your friends and acquaintances show some appreciation for what they are seeing. Perhaps, most importantly, having exhibitions exposes me to a wide range of people with whom I can communicate and engage in dialogue about art as well as life in general. Those who are curious about art are almost invariably open minded and interesting folks from whom there is much that I can learn.

My Approach to Photography Changes

For several years, I joined outdoor photography workshops that visited the dramatic national parks and other spectacular parts of America's far west. Invariably, in these workshops, you emerge from your room around 5 a.m. to catch a fleeting glimpse of the rising sun before returning, half dazed from sleep deprivation, for breakfast. That is hardly my preferred way of starting the day. There were usually six or seven others in the workshop, and all were passionate nature photographers. We followed the leader's itinerary. He knew the best places to shoot and the best times to go (and we were paying him for this, of course).

It seems that almost everyone starts out as a nature photographer. You can only photograph Yosemite's Half Dome or the red rocks of Sedona so many times before the realization hits you that these sights have been shot by plenty of others over the years, and the scenery that captivates you has become almost a cliché. Do you really think that your efforts will surpass those of your predecessors and that viewers will be excited to see yet another representation of a numbingly familiar scene? I doubt it. And it is not that fascinating, at least to me, to walk in the footsteps of others as you try to capture a different perspective or wait for the emergence of some magical sunlight.

My approach to photography has always been highly instinctual. I shoot what moves me, what makes me excited. If I am not excited by what I shoot, then why on earth am I shooting whatever it is that is in front of me? Art is about stirring the emotions, of both the artist and the viewer, and it is through these emotions that we connect with one another. Communicating our feelings is, I believe, the name of the game.

Gradually, without consciously realizing it, I was becoming drawn more and more to abstract imagery. Because the nature of the subject is often not clear with abstract art, each person sees the work differently and can assign their own interpretations and meanings to it. Naturally, that stimulates the mind as well as the senses. My hope is that the piece comes to resemble a painting rather than a photograph, and some viewers truly believe it to be the latter! If so, goal achieved! Abstract art, of course, is not everyone's taste and that is fine with me!

OK, Let's Look at Some of this Abstract Photography

First, let's throw in a realistic landscape: "Sand Dunes, Death Valley." As I wandered around these wide expanses of sand, getting more and more disoriented and potentially lost it could, I suppose, have been the death of me. I was looking for intersecting lines and their patterns. They were not that easy to come by! However, I finally found what I was searching for. Those curving lines of sand, and their shadows, were the scene's appeal. Slightly sensuous, perhaps? Anyway, it is probably my favorite landscape shot.

Fast forward several years, and I'm becoming abstract: "Wiggly Lines." What is this about? I never let the title give the subject away! Those broad, wiggly lines were reflections of the masts of a boat, wiggling because of a slight current. But would you know if I did not tell you? Maybe, maybe not. Either way, it is okay with me.

"Suffocating Spider" is another reflection, but of what? Again, we're in the water, but looking at a more unusual sight, this time of a tropical plant. Those radiating strands kept changing with the flow of water. It could, I suppose, have been any insect of your choice. Since the reflection was constantly changing, I just kept shooting. If one did not work, then perhaps the next one would. You never know.

When I watch these reflections, I am in a dream world. What I see plays games with my imagination; it doesn't matter what it really is. With so many varying interpretations, it should come as no surprise that others find elements within the photograph that I am completely unaware of, such as faces, other body parts or perhaps a flower.

Another abstract genre that I explore, and increasingly so, is "Intentional Camera Movement." This imposing title merely indicates that you move the camera during a long exposure, and this movement obviously blurs the subject. The faster you move the camera, the more abstract the image becomes. It is very experimental, for you are never quite sure what the effect will be, and so you take lots and lots of shots. The ensuing effect is even more painterly than that created by reflections.

"Blowing in the Wind" could be a lock of hair, a dog's tail or even a fattened letter of a new alphabet, but it is none of the above for it is a piece of blown glass on a black background. Whatever! Just enjoy the shape and its implied movement, and finish downing the last drops of your glass of wine as you try to make sense of it.

Finally, there's "Ghostly." I'm sure you can recognize that these are people, but people doing what? Are they coal miners who are lost, folks praying at a funeral, or troops readying themselves for battle? No, they are not. They are a group of dancers on stage. They are moving, as seems to be the tendency with dancers these days, so the effect is even more unpredictable. Shooting dance always has a delightfully unpredictable element, unless you know the piece backwards.

All I ask is that you allow yourself to be transported into a different world. Every piece of art evokes a different reaction, perhaps even a negative reaction! I used to be afraid of abstract art, for I did not know what to make of it and so I felt foolish…but not anymore. Abstract art is now making huge strides in the popularity stakes, especially among the younger generation. So why not give it a chance?

Our Grandchildren: From Babies to Toddlers

We visited Philadelphia several times a year as our grandchildren were growing out of the early baby phase, although Covid lurking around the corner sometimes thwarted our plans. Every time we saw them, they sprouted new, endearing characteristics. We never knew what to expect!

Quinn was a thoughtful and sensitive soul. We could tell that he was very aware of his surroundings and did not always jump immediately into action. Eve, on the other hand, was always on the go, bursting with enthusiasm and

Sand Dunes, Death Valley

Wiggly Lines

Suffocating Spider

Blowing in the Wind

Ghostly

quite uninhibited. There was a striking difference between their two personalities, and always such fun to see how they interacted and responded to our presence. Anne was "Gigi" and I was "Papa."

Early on, Quinn showed a love for music. He had a great sense of rhythm and "played" a variety of children's musical instruments including the drums and guitar. Jesse was a devotee of Bruce Springsteen and quite musical himself. Many evenings, we were treated to a show by the two of them. Jesse would sing a Springsteen song, and Quinn would follow along, banging his drums or strumming his guitar. He would sometimes add his voice to that of Jesse. Those shows were a real treat!

Eve was irrepressible, and possessed with boundless energy. She was forever changing her clothes, and we became used to seeing different versions of herself coming down the stairs every day. She was strong and very athletic, with an amazing sense of balance until she finally fell over. She would then pick herself up and carry on as if nothing had happened.

Both of our grandchildren attended a very well-run private preschool. They painted and drew, made friends with other children, and clearly enjoyed their time. They quickly developed a vocabulary. Each time we visited, new words and phrases would pop out of their mouths. They were obviously bright eyed and bushy tailed, and very much on the ball.

Elizabeth and Jesse were quick to introduce them to sporting activities. They were avid scooters (scooterers?) and loved to scoot or walk to one of the large playgrounds for children in the neighborhood, filled with slides, climbing opportunities, and swings. Elizabeth started to hit tennis balls with Quinn and Jesse found time to play baseball or basketball with him. When they visited us, David and I introduced Quinn to golf, and Elizabeth has continued to keep him involved with the sport. It was not long before both children were on skis on nearby bunny slopes. Eve started ballet lessons at a very young age and clearly was going to follow in her mother's footsteps. Both of our grandchildren have so many opportunities to have lots of fun!

Interlude: Ponderings on Art, Artists, and Angst

Obviously, artists create art. But what is art? Rembrandt was an artist, for sure; no one will deny that. How about randomly splashing paint onto a canvas? That is action painting and was made famous by Jackson Pollock. One of his paintings sold for $140 million in 2006. I have a really hard time understanding that! Marcel Duchamp thought it was for artists to decide what was and what was not a work of art. He presented an upside-down urinal as art; it was one of his first "ready-mades" and it changed the art world and how we see art forever.

The Oxford English Dictionary (OED) includes, in its definition of art: "Skill; its display or application." Well, that is a pretty broad definition. Does this then include the art of fly fishing for tasty trout to eat at dinner, the art of wiping out a tribal nation such as the Cherokees, and the art of carrying out the Spanish Inquisition? Perhaps I am being unfair to the OED, so I will back off and consider the much less expansive definition, namely that of the more classical creative arts.

The creative arts obviously include a variety of expressive forms: painting, music, architecture and literature are just a few that come to mind. So, how do we decide into which we plunge? You can spend an awful lot of time chasing rainbows only to find out that you've come up against a rather solid brick wall. We have all been there, I think. It often does not work when we are pushed by well-meaning parents, for they cannot see inside our heads (or souls). Like many good little boys and girls, I was expected to play the piano. I had no aptitude for this and did not find pounding the black and white keys at all enjoyable so I (belatedly) said goodbye to my piano teacher. My father did the same, shortly after covering his teacher's piano stool with ink. Nicely done, dad!

I think it is good if we can find a form of expression that turns us on, that we feel passionate about. It does not really matter what we select, although I personally do not go for violent choices. If we become passionate about our selection, we have probably hit a home run. At work, our enjoyment or passion can vary greatly. I suspect many accountants do not like crunching numbers all the time, whereas professional truffle hunters (yes, they do exist!) may be completely carried away by the difficulties and rewards of their efforts. But, outside of work, the world is our oyster. I believe that we are all creative beings, but many of us do not know it until we find an outlet that works for us. Maybe you will come to love basket weaving, sculpting or possibly even organizing crab races. See what art form is up your street, even if it takes two or three attempts to find out. Don't be too anxious. A small dose of angst never hurt anyone. It is well worth the effort!

Anne and I go to India!

Why on earth did we go to India, unless it was to catch dysentery or dengue or some other nasty infection? Or maybe malaria if you did not take those antimalarial tablets that Donald Trump was so fond of. So why go? Because it is a totally fascinating country, although not one where you can be footloose and fancy free.

Choosing a company for such a trip was not easy. However, I came across one, India Odyssey Tours, that had rave reviews. Those reviews, however, were only about one-day trips from Delhi! The company was based in China and had expanded its operations into India and other parts of Asia. I contacted them and received an immediate reply from a Bunny Zhao, who became our travel consultant. She explained that the company arranged private tours for small groups, offered flexible itineraries, and arranged different local guides in each city on our route.

This approach seemed ideal and, together with our friends Doug Day and Laryn Peterson, we (or, rather I, with some trepidation) went ahead with planning a trip to Delhi and Rajasthan, which was the jewel of the Mughal Empire. The Mughals were descendants of Genghis Khan and Tamerlane and built magnificent palaces and forts in Rajasthan between the 16th and 18th centuries. The Taj Mahal was the most famous of these lavishly ornate palaces.

The ruling Mughals were very tolerant of the Hindu majority, some of whom reached high positions in their courts. We saw the famed cities of Jaipur, Jodhpur and Udaipur, but, for me, the most moving experience of all was the visit to the Jain Temple at Ranakpur.

This temple was a huge, highly decorated building in the middle of nowhere. Beware, though, if you are wearing leather or are a menstruating woman, as you are then not supposed to enter. How are they checking, though? Jains believe in reincarnation and that all living things, even plants, have souls. There was a feeling of seriousness and austerity inside the temple, greatly reinforced by the dignity of the monks. Despite my overriding irreligiosity, I found myself greatly moved by the somber devotion of the followers of Jainism we saw inside the temple. People of other faiths would, I think, be very impressed by the quiet and calm purity that you sensed everywhere.

In complete contrast was the Chandni Chowk bazaar in Old Delhi: a chaotic market lined by hawkers and porters, with narrow alleyways and an incomprehensible, tangled mess of telephone and other wires crisscrossing above the streets. Rickshaws were everywhere, as well as other forms of transport that beggared description. Guys hung out on the street hoping for a day's work, and one or two barbers were in action, blade in hand, at the curbside. India was a tapestry of enormous complexity, where chaos and purity lay side by side. It was a huge nation of very different people enduring hard lives with enormous dignity.

Teaching High School Photography: An Opportunity Out of the Blue

When I had an exhibition at the home of the Indianapolis Symphony Orchestra, I was introduced to Heather Teets, the director of fine arts at Park Tudor School, a private school widely regarded as the best in Indiana. There, I taught intermediate photography for two fall semesters. My main issue turned out to be the technical side of conveying information, rather than the subject of photography itself. I bought a Mac laptop, needed to learn how to make PowerPoint presentations, and master other bells and whistles that were technical in nature.

It was a wonderful experience that required a lot of preparation but was very satisfying. There were many students who were very gifted artistically, some far more than me, and were great fun to teach. Since I had never formally studied photography, my goal was to convey my passion to them and, at first, encourage them to shoot whatever it was that moved them. Of course, I then moved on to other aspects of the art form such as black and white photography, street photography, and abstract photography. Fortunately, Heather had given me her outline of what she had previously taught during this course. It came in very useful!

A colleague at Park Tudor, Joe Fumusa, who taught social studies and U.S. government, befriended me and gave me a permanent invitation to sit in on his classes. I felt very honored, for I was the only adult allowed to join them. This had a strong impact on me. He always emphasized that memorization and grading were unimportant; his goal was to encourage students to grapple with ideas and to be able to support their views in class without resorting to notes or texts. They had to think on their feet. I had been brought up to memorize everything, so this was a rather new experience for me. I found it enthralling.

Being at Park Tudor gave me the opportunity to mix and socialize with teachers of other subjects at the school, which was often quite stimulating. Halfway through the semester, I was asked to give a talk to the student body and their parents in an "Artist's Series." The previous speaker was a Hollywood "B" film director. He was a very polished speaker and therefore a hard act to follow! I put a lot of effort into preparing this talk, for he had set the bar very high, and I did not want to knock it down. I illustrated my voyage to date in photography, and somehow, managed to acquit myself reasonably well.

David: A Multifaceted Guy

For a long time, David and I had wanted to indulge in a father/son golf trip to Scotland and, finally, in 2017, it happened. We stayed in bed and breakfasts. One of the owners gave us particularly useful local advice. When we came to St. Andrews, where we had been unable to secure a tee time, he advised us to show up and report to the starter, who duly noted our names. The starter first informed us that there was a possibility of teeing off around 5:30 p.m. (it stays light late there) but, after about an hour spent lolling around on the adjacent putting green, he suddenly informed us that we could start in five minutes. What a lucky break! We also played, among other courses, at Carnoustie (tough in driving rain), Gleneagles (very snooty), and Royal Dornoch (an unrecognized gem) in the far north. Golf had always glued us together, and this was a very memorable bonding experience.

Anne and I visited David in Houston, or he came to spend time with us, especially at Christmas. He also enjoyed staying with Elizabeth and family in Philadelphia. The grandchildren really adored their "Uncle David." Whether in Houston or Philadelphia, we always relished these times.

A few years ago, David decided to head for Ecuador to climb one of the world's highest active volcanoes, Cotopaxi. Reaching a height of 19,300 feet, it is no piece of cake. Indeed, one of the three climbers with David was sent down before summiting, as he was not in good enough shape to continue. Some climbers have even fallen to their death on its slopes. At 18,500 feet, our lad was suddenly overcome by an urge to empty his bowels. He had to remove his harness, attend to his business, and then re-harness, no easy feat at this elevation. Nevertheless, he made it to the top and back without much further difficulty.

What else does David do in his spare time? Not much at all, except hiking, skiing, playing tennis and golf, cooking and making sure he does not fall asleep at the wheel of his Tesla. There's never a dull moment!

Interlude: How much Vitamin Sea is needed for me?

But which Vitamin Sea? Vitamin C matters greatly; everyone needs it. According to the Mayo Clinic, it protects your cells against free radicals. Radicals?

They want to change us, change society, change everything. And how? By revolution, of course. Yes, by revolution. Vitamin C has been with us a long time, though it is hardly revolutionary.

Assuming I am well supplied with Vitamin C, it is the other "C" I am after. I just wish I lived by the sea; ponds in Indiana don't really cut it for me. How can a pond invigorate you? I cannot wait to get back to the coast. It is so liberating and dreamlike, just to watch the waves or gaze into the unknown in the distance.

On Vancouver Island's west coast lies a small town, Tofino. Only one road leads there and it is a six-hour drive from the island's main city, Victoria. People venture there for its wild coastline and laid-back nature. Many come to surf, others to enjoy its almost deserted beaches and dramatic coastal trails. Tofino's small harbors are filled with fishing boats and suchlike. There are no sleek, fancy yachts. Tofino was where I first fell in love with reflections, ever-changing reflections of the boats moored in the small harbor there. These reflections, when the sun is out, create magical effects.

It was my good friend Giles Stevenson who first told me about Tofino. Giles and I alternate between annual visits to each other's homes (at least that was the case until Covid hit). He lives in Victoria on Vancouver Island, which is home to some stunning golf courses. When we golf here in Indianapolis, the scenery is far more subdued, but it matters not because we get together primarily to enjoy good company. We have, over the years, gotten to know each other's families and friends to add to this enjoyment. Our golf is nothing to brag about, but it is a great excuse to perpetuate our relationship!

Adventures in Patagonia

Patagonia sounded wild, and I wanted to go. Browsing on the Internet, it was clear that local, rather than American, travel agents would be better informed about arranging travel to such a remote destination. Somehow, I stumbled across Wangulen Odyssey Tours, a two-man operation run by Felipe Soto, a Chilean, and his partner Perry McIntosh who was from Midland, Texas. I contacted Felipe and he called me back immediately. It was soon clear that he was attentive to every detail and passionate about the whole traveling experience. I was a little disconcerted to learn that my entire trip would be based on vouchers, but he assured me that this would work fine.

The exciting part of the trip started in Chile's Lake District, where Perry and Felipe met me. They drove me to a restaurant halfway up the snow-capped slopes of Osorno, an 8,700-foot volcano that dominates the landscape far into the distance. They waited in the restaurant while I walked around part of the volcano's perimeter for almost an hour at an altitude of about 4,000 feet. Since I did not want my kind hosts to be kept waiting too long, I adopted a relatively brisk pace. The next day, I joined a boat journey across Lake Todos de Los Santos. For most of that trip, Osorno was staring us in the face. Later, this splendid backdrop was replaced by dramatic views of the nearby steep Andean mountains.

Several days afterwards, I was deep in Patagonia. The tour guide suggested a walk to see some icebergs floating in a nearby lagoon. We crossed a rickety wooden bridge with netting to hold onto for safety. The bridge swayed in the howling wind and only six or seven people were allowed on the bridge at one time. Once on the shores of the lagoon, I was being blown sideways and removed my spectacles to avoid them flying away! Back on the bus, I asked the guide about the wind. She said it was about 100 kilometers an hour (60 miles per hour), which seemed quite mind boggling.

Later, I arrived at 6:30 a.m. at the local bus station to jump on a bus that would take us on the seven-hour journey across the border into El Calafate, Argentina. The bus station was large, very confusing, and no one spoke English. Finally, after waving my voucher in every possible direction, I located the correct bus and clambered on board.

The next day was beautifully sunny, and we headed out to the Perito Moreno Glacier. It is easy to be overawed by this glacier for it is 19 miles long, bigger than Buenos Aires. It is one of the few glaciers in the world that is actually growing! We first saw it from multiple balconies, from which we could appreciate the glacier's massive termination towering 90 yards above the waters of Lake Argentine. We then took a one-hour boat trip to gaze close up at the amazing sight of the glacier plunging into the icy waters below, with its sharply jagged peaks rising immediately above us. The experience was surreal.

On the way back I felt lousy. I was breathing hard, and discovered that I had ankle edema. Clearly, I was sliding into heart failure, for the first time since my massive heart attack 10 years ago. Lack of sleep, walking too far at 4,000 feet and a demanding schedule were probably all contributory factors. This was scary, since the last thing I wanted to do was go to a local hospital where the doctors probably did not speak much English and would have a hard time understanding my complex cardiac history. I phoned Anne, who called my cardiologist Doug Pitts. His solution was simple: take a diuretic, furosemide (Lasix). Fortunately, I was able to buy the stuff over the counter without needing to see a doctor. Two days later, I regained my former health and felt fine.

Elizabeth's and Jesse's Plates are Full

You must be a juggler to handle all that Elizabeth and Jesse do! For starters, both have hung out their shingles. Elizabeth has a solo practice of family law in and around Philadelphia, which she pursues diligently and without fanfare. Fortunately, she can work mainly from home. Jesse is in practice with his brother Brendan Klaproth, whose office is in Washington, D.C. I greatly love Jesse, respect his intellect, and know that you do not want to be on the opposite side when he takes a case!

They are terrific parents. Elizabeth is a very devoted mother to Quinn (now six) and Eve (now four). She carefully supervises their activities and encourages them in every possible way. They are lucky to have her as their mother! They have no household help, so Elizabeth does all the cooking and shopping as well as much else. Elizabeth tries to go to the nearby gym every day, and Jesse fills in to make this possible. Occasionally, very occasionally, she goes into Manhattan to see her favorite ballet company, the New York City Ballet. She and my cousin Susan Schaier have developed a meaningful relationship, and they do manage to meet from time to time.

Living in downtown Philadelphia is not the easiest of places to bring up children. Recently, Elizabeth and Jesse joined a club on the outskirts of Philadelphia, Germantown Cricket Club, to which they sometimes escape. Elizabeth plays tennis on grass courts there, and Quinn is now following suit. Both our grandchildren enjoy playing with Jesse, including "not too rough" rough house. Jesse's time spent on law cases can be demanding. With much at stake, a lot of preparation is needed. Nevertheless he, too, is very involved with the children.

We love going to Philadelphia to see them all, and it helps that Philadelphia is such a charming city. Most of the restaurants and shops are privately owned, and there are almost no chain stores. We know the neighborhoods very well by now. It is almost like we live there! If only they were not so far away.

Interlude: Is Being a Jew Good for You?

In the absence of any Jewish ritual at home, attending Hebrew evening class as a young child was like being led blindfolded into an entirely new world. Not surprisingly, I was quite disinterested in learning this weird new language of my forefathers. It was not a helpful introduction to my religion, however well intended.

As time went on, I learned that belonging to God's chosen race was no joyride. The deep-seated rot about the Jews started with Constantine, the Roman emperor. In 315 CE, he issued an edict that described Jews as a dangerous and abominable sect, and if they dared attack or show anger to a Christian, they "must speedily be given to flames and burn." It was not until 1998 CE that Pope John Paul II, undoubtedly one of the greatest figures of the 20th century, famously asked for forgiveness for the acts committed by Christians against the Jews.

Almost 1,700 years of society's unceasing hatred of Jews seems rather a long time and the story is by no means over. It has now become increasingly popular to equate antisemitism with anti-Zionism. This does not hold water. Many Jews in Israel have questioned the policy of expanding settlements in the West Bank, but that does not make them antisemites.

When Wall Street Journal journalist Daniel Pearl was brutally decapitated by terrorists in Pakistan on February 21, 2002, his last words were: "My father is Jewish, my mother is Jewish, I am Jewish." Note that he described his background but made no mention whatsoever of religion. For some unfathomable reason, many Christians, Muslims, and other religions do not seem to understand this duality. Perhaps, without their religion, they feel unsteady on their feet. That is too bad because it is their problem, and they have made it a problem for us.

Strasbourg: An Idyllic City

In September 2019, shortly before Covid hit, Anne and I took a Rhine (and wine) cruise. Although the boat was always on the German side of the river, if you crossed over the bridge, you would find yourself in France. While we enjoyed many cities along the way, Strasbourg was definitely my favorite.

Although in France, this more than 2,000-year-old-city in Alsace Lorraine has a distinctive culture that is very much its own. The historic center of Strasbourg, The Grande Ile (a UNESCO World Heritage site), is an island essentially devoid of any means of transport except for bicycles or your own two feet. As a result, the pace of life slows down and you can take your time savoring its medieval beauty. We had lunch with a German couple (the city has long been tossed backwards and forwards between Germany and France). They commented that, when you crossed into nearby Germany, everything took place at a far greater speed.

While Strasbourg has a famous cathedral, I found its cobbled side streets, picturesque half-timbered houses and winding canals to be far more inviting. "La Petite France," with its many channels of water, is particularly charming. Its name was not chosen for patriotic or architectural reasons. It comes from the "hospice of the syphilitic" which was built there in the fifteenth century to cure persons afflicted with syphilis, then called the "French disease." I cannot help suspecting that the French may have given this disease a Teutonic causation at times in the city's tumultuous past.

The city has many modern touches and elegant shops mixed in among its medieval buildings. I could have hung out for weeks in this enchanting place, but we were on a cruise that limited our stay. I hope to be back there one day, for we barely touched its surface. The rest of the cruise included many other fascinating cities, but, nevertheless, Strasbourg stood out head and shoulders above all the others.

Other Countries that I (or We) Managed to Visit

After retiring, I (or Anne and I) had plenty of time to visit other countries, in addition to the ones already mentioned. But I will not bore you with the details of the diaries of these trips (even though I've kept them). I could put them in chronological order, list them for each continent, or place them in my order of preference. Instead, I will mention them in alphabetical order and let you know what fascinated me the most in each of them. Okay?

Costa Rica: Rainforests, birds and more birds, wildlife (monkeys, crocodiles etc), beaches

Croatia: Dubrovnik (old city), Island of Korcula, magnificent coastline

Germany: Heidelberg (castle, Neckar River), Cologne (cathedral), Rhine cruise, castles galore
Jordan: Petra, of course
Portugal: Douro Valley, port and more port, Lisbon (Alfama old district)
Thailand: Buddhist temples and their gold leaf … do not touch, Koh Phi Phi Islands
Turkey: Istanbul (Hagia Sophia; mosque turned museum), Cappadocia's fairy chimneys
Vietnam: Mekong Delta and floating market, Hue (Imperial City)

Now that we are in this COVID era, who knows when overseas travel will again become so easy? I'm so glad that we had the opportunity to see so much before the virus struck!

Freddie and the Church of the Holy Sepulcher

When on a guided tour, I have frequently lost touch with my group and this is inevitably related to my desire to hang around and take more photographs. Here is one striking example.

The Church of the Holy Sepulcher in Jerusalem is perhaps the holiest church in Christendom, for it is where Christ was believed to have been crucified, died, and later resurrected. This massive building houses six competing denominations: the Catholics, the Greek Orthodox, the Armenian Orthodox, the Syrian Orthodox, the Copts and the Ethiopian Orthodox. I feel badly for the Ethiopians, for they have lost out badly. They have no territory inside the church, as their territory is strictly limited to part of the church's rooftop.

The Greek Orthodox and the Armenians, in particular, have engaged in many fights over their respective rights. When our guide took us inside the church, there were hundreds of pilgrims and tourists all over the place. While there, I witnessed a Greek Orthodox priest start to beat up a pilgrim. After watching this unruly spectacle, I pushed my way through the crowds, and saw an elderly Armenian woman bending down over a slab of stone and repeatedly kissing it. She was wearing a bright yellow headscarf. Naturally, I had to photograph her. I was so entranced that I took many photographs, as well as of many others humbly engaged in similar acts of supplication.

Accordingly, I lost all track of time. When I finally emerged from the church, my group was nowhere to be seen. There were crowds everywhere. It was at least ten minutes before our guide found me, grabbed me by the arm and dragged me back into the group. But it was worth it, for I had my pictures!

Interlude: If Music be the Feast of Life, Play On

My father, as you know, was Viennese. In the early twentieth century, Vienna was bursting with intellectual ideas. He attended some lectures given by Alfred Adler, the well-known psychoanalyst. During one, he met a young lady who frequently took him to see the Vienna State Opera. This was his introduction to classical music, for which he never lost his love.

About nine years ago, I went to the Fourth of July parade in Carmel. A brass band was playing, conducted by Tom Akins who had been the principal tympanist for the Indianapolis Symphony Orchestra (ISO). He graciously allowed me to take close-up photographs of the musicians and their gleaming instruments. The photographs must have impressed him, for he subsequently interviewed me twice on his radio show (twice? ...you've got to be kidding!). Not only that, but he suggested to the marketing director of the ISO that I should be invited to photograph some of the symphony's performances.

This opportunity was quite an honor, for the symphony had several paid professional photographers on their books (I was, of course, more than thrilled to shoot "pro bono"). The highlight of these experiences came when Mario Venzago, the former conductor of the orchestra, who had been unceremoniously fired by the previous C.E.O., was invited back by the C.E.O.'s successor. I was asked to shoot not only his return appearance with our orchestra, but also to capture the unveiling of a portrait of him at a reception following the performance, a painting that should have been presented before his ignominious departure.

The maestro had been hugely popular with our audiences. He exuded a warmth and charm on the stage (after all, he did come from the Italian part of Switzerland!), and it had always endeared him to us. For the performance, I was told that it was imperative to get shots of him as he turned to gratefully acknowledge the packed house. Since he received a prolonged standing ovation, it was very easy for me to make my way through the crowd to obtain the requisite images.

Although I have no musical talent whatsoever, I very much love classical music: Mozart's piano concertos, Verdi's operatic arias and haunting pieces of Mahler's works are all special favorites of mine. That evening at the symphony was a magical one in which I got to witness and document our delayed tribute to this unique and wonderful man. It was an experience that I will never forget, and was a veritable feast for my eyes.

Anne: Definitely the Better Half of Our Marriage

Anne and I find plenty to do, even though the paths that we take during the day are quite different. Anne is very involved in community activities. She is very active in her church and its food kitchen, previously helped patients in the hospice, provided dog therapy for hospitalized patients, and much else. On top of all these activities, she is a dedicated piano student, and takes great care of me. I am very grateful for I would not do at all well if left to fare for myself!

We enjoy spending time playing golf, going to symphony concerts, theater productions and dance performances. She loves to ski and goes to Colorado (or nearby) twice a year to enjoy the sport with the Ski Club of Indianapolis. She is also a keen bicyclist, and brave enough to do Pilates.

Anne has great discipline in almost anything to which she applies herself. This, in turn, requires dedication and determination. She is not deflected from completing a task, whether it is working for the good of the community or the good of her family. In contrast to her, I am easily distracted, and have limited attention span coupled with a highly impulsive nature.

I reserve even more admiration for Anne's practical skills. She knows how things work, and rapidly carries out all manner of functions around and outside the house. Give me an object with two or more buttons, and I become easily confused as to which to hit. A vending machine for soft drinks, for example, can fox my best attempts to deliver a Coke or Sprite. You want other examples? Well, who else has poured engine oil into the carburetor, or manual dishwasher fluid into a dish washer? The former required a phone call to have my car towed, and the latter resulted in immediate rental of a specialized vacuum cleaner to handle the copious foam engulfing the kitchen floor. And that is only for starters.

I also admire that Anne is calm and unflappable. She does not allow events to ruffle her feathers. Calmness is not my strong suit. As a medical student, when I rotated through psychiatry, I was relieved to discover that my only medical malady was a mild chronic anxiety state. I still do, so I haven't yet been able to replicate Anne's relaxed state of mind, and probably never will.

New Friends, Old Friends, and More

More opportunities arise for developing friendships, as well as hobbies, if you are no longer reading those X-rays. And, as you advance in years, reacquainting with old friends becomes more meaningful.

Tom and Shirley Mueller became very good friends with me about seven years ago. Tom, a retired cardiologist, is a fellow photographer, but far more skilled technically. However, since we shoot such different subjects, this is of little consequence. We get together at least once a week when he is in town and will chat about almost anything as well as look at each other's photographs. He's amazingly knowledgeable but does not flaunt his intellect at all.

Shirley, his wife, has a fascinating background. Having been an academic neurologist, then an investment advisor, and now an internationally recognized expert on Chinese export porcelains, attests to her mastery of very different fields of endeavor. A book she recently wrote, "Inside the Head of a Collector: Neuropsychological Forces at Play," blends her knowledge of collecting (porcelain) with scientific insights into how our brains respond to art. Because of her unique set of skills, she is supremely qualified to address this fascinating and complex subject.

Other good friends include Claudia and Irwin Labin. Claudia has a very outgoing personality and is now a talented multimedia artist. Previously, she was a gifted playwright and short-story writer. Quite an artistic all-rounder! Irwin, her husband, is a skilled metal sculptor and the guy who regularly beats me at chess when I show up online. The Mueller's, Labin's and Anne and I often get together to eat and drink wherever our fancy takes us.

It has been great to renew with old friends from Leeds: Bernard Olsburgh, James Denton, John Dyson, and David Apfel. Another guy from Leeds, Harvey Fish, who I did not know until we met in a Haifa flea market (!), is a superb street photographer. His work is in the same league as Henri Cartier-Bresson!

I continue golfing with enthusiasm, but not always to great effect. Previously, I had golfed a great deal with Patrick Bourdillon and Jonas Rydberg. Now I am golfing in an "oldies" group at Broadmoor with Bill Claymon, Bob Silbert, and George McAdoo. While our camaraderie is strong, our golf is clearly not. When I golf with Anne, Faith (our sister-in-law) often joins us. Anne stresses that they are not competing against each other; nevertheless, they both carefully keep note of their strokes! Paul Schmidt (a true scholar) and I have played alternately at Crooked Stick and Broadmoor. That is always a pleasure.

The Entrancement of Akko

Yes, Jerusalem, Tel Aviv, and the Dead Sea are tourist "musts" but give me Akko any day. I was lucky enough to stay there twice with Eytan Hurwitz, who, despite being Jewish, is very much loved by the Arab citizens of old Akko (Acre). He knows almost every inch of this ancient Crusader city, with its beautiful archways and maze of sidestreets, and he delighted in showing me its unrivaled sights. A day with Eytan in Akko is like a day with no one else. What do I mean? Okay, I will chronicle just one day: Tunisian synagogue, clock repair man at work lying on his back because room was so cramped, charismatic ancient Arab serving every imaginable tea next to a carpark, alleyways where everyone greeted him, murals he had painted for the old city, and dumpster diving on way home. With this generous, multi-talented artist there is never a dull moment, nothing is predictable, and everything is unique.

Seeing a city such as Akko with its long and rich history in the inspired hands of Eytan is a remarkable experience. His next door neighbors are Arab and their son is confined to a wheelchair by severe congenital physical and mental disorders. Despite this, his eyes light up every time he sees Eytan and they are clearly very good friends. Eytan's spirit and generosity are truly legion.

Ballet Austin Comes to Akko

In 2013, the entire company of Ballet Austin came to Akko for five days, financed largely by Austin's Jewish population. Why? They came to perform a Holocaust ballet, "Light: The Holocaust and Humanities Project." The Jewish Partnership agreed to my request to photograph the rehearsal and performance, along with two other photographers. Words cannot do justice to what we saw. We watched, spellbound. The dancers were engulfed in portraying the stark horrors of the victims by the intensity of their movements and body language. The music was haunting and, when called for, piercing. The costumes were sparse and, in the concentration camp scenes, nude in color. Nothing was left to the imagination. You, the audience, were there on stage suffering with them.

This work was only performed in cities willing to organize wide-ranging community discussions about discrimination, hatred and bigotry in all its varied manifestations, including bullying, gender discrimination, and attacks on gays and lesbians. The intent is that people in the community will come to feel a sense of responsibility to speak out whenever they see or hear such hate-filled activities. This experience changed my views about our obligations in life, and I tell as many people as possible about its impact on me, in the hopes that they will feel the same. When I do so, my voice cracks and I am sometimes close to tears.

At a later date, I had an exhibition of photographs of the performance at the Jewish Community Center in Austin, and shared the stage with both the company's artistic director, Stephen Mills, and its executive director, Cookie Ruiz. I felt very honored to be asked to exhibit and address the audience there. Ballet Austin went on to perform the Holocaust ballet in both Tel Aviv and Jerusalem. In the latter city, they performed in the auditorium specifically built for the trial of Adolf Eichmann. How ironic!

A Swastika Lands in our Neighborhood

In June 18, 2018, a swastika and iron crosses were spray-painted onto two walls of a brick shed on the grounds of Shaarey Tefilla synagogue, located just one mile away from our home in Carmel. It was terrifying to believe that such a despicable act could happen almost on one's own doorstep. The community was outraged at this horrendous vandalism. Their response was to call for a meeting of religious and civic leaders in the main auditorium of the synagogue. More than 1,000 people showed up, and religious leaders of all persuasions as well as the mayor of Carmel addressed the audience. Only the mayor brought up a warning of the horrors associated with that symbol of Nazism in Germany, reminding the audience that the same scenario could, one day, unfold here. The religious leaders, to their credit, all strongly emphasized their solidarity and unity with their Jewish counterparts.

There has been, of late, a resurgence of antisemitism both in the United States and in many European countries. In recent years, French Jews have left for Israel in record numbers. In Britain, Jeremy Corbyn, who led the opposition Labor party in 2019, was openly antisemitic, and Jews there feared greatly for their safety. Fortunately, he lost the election that year. Certainly, I feel safer in the United States but antisemitism here is spreading and has been aggravated by the emergence of white supremacists and their crackpot theories. The swastika in our neighborhood came as a shocking reminder of our continuing vulnerability to such acts of provocation.

There is an understandable reluctance on the part of other religions to discuss antisemitism, but it would be far healthier for all of us if we could calmly and openly address this longstanding issue. I am hesitant to bring up the subject for serious discussion with anyone unless they are close friends, for I realize that I may be treading on eggshells. Increasingly, though, I feel the need to speak up. As Ritu Ghatourey, the noted Indian author said: "The world suffers a lot, not because of the violence of bad people, but because of the silence of good people." Clearly, she and Stephen Mills, along with so many others, are reading from the same page.

Closing Reflections

I am still not sure where I belong, as I do not steadfastly adhere to the culture of any one community. I have been told something different; namely that I belong to a community of outsiders. That, though, seems a nebulous concept. For sure, I now recognize and am truly proud of my Jewish origins, but I do not feel the need to be cocooned within that societal web. I am very hesitant to bow to any kind of authoritarianism, whether religious or not. Strict obedience to authority greatly limits my personal freedom.

Identity change is a complicated business. It is one thing to cease practicing Jewish ritual and leave the Jewish community, but quite another to change my name and way of life and then become absorbed into very different communities. Frequent changes of location, including moving to a different country, only serve to increase the feeling of being a nomad. On the other hand, the shifting landscapes and communities have been the source of much excitement and have given rise to a far more varied and interesting life than would have been the case if I had remained in Leeds.

Since retiring, my mind has been opened and I see a world of people that need to respect each other. Mere tolerance is definitely not going to be enough. Nationalism, however, is rife and mutual respect is falling more and more under the gun. We have dealt our offspring a disturbing set of cards in which suspicion, populism, and alternate facts increasingly rule the day. We must hope that our children will right the boat, and there are promising signs that they will, but this will likely take at least one or two decades to implement, given the ever-increasing polarization with which we are now faced.

Looking back at my life, I realize that I was consumed by my career for far too long. I never intended to be engulfed in the way that I was, and to find myself paying so little attention to my family. Swimming in many different waters, though, did place unexpected demands on me. In my early days, I thought that it would be fine to just be a radiologist somewhere in the south of England, but the wind blew me far further afield.

I am very happy that I have widened my horizons since retiring. Meeting people through photography has played a large part in this. Seeing our grandchildren grow up is a marvelous experience, and I have a wonderful wife and two great children. I want to be around to see how our grandchildren's personalities develop and how they will grow in many different directions. I hope that they have open, curious minds and do not hang back when opportunities arise! Above all, I hope they will be far less discriminating against others than has been the case with my generation.

I will keep shooting with my camera, and hope we can start to travel safely and more widely since being hit by Covid, for traveling has always fed my brain. I am happy to stay here in Carmel where Anne and I have good friends and where there are signs of growing diversity. I just need to stay healthy, keep swimming and doing (albeit reluctantly) my exercises.

There is a part of me that will always be restless and curious. Being an urban nomad has led me to have a fascinating, ever-changing life despite its uncertainties, and I would not have had it otherwise. My experiences have been many and varied, and I have encountered more than my fair share of interesting people. If I have any useful advice to give, it would be to avoid complacency at all costs and to try and keep an open mind. Life should be an adventure!

Acknowledgements

I was encouraged by friends to write this memoir. Initially, there was some reluctancy on my part; while my parents' circumstances in Austria were – to my mind – fascinating and compelling, I did not think my life to be particularly extraordinary. Giles Stevenson, and others, gave me food for thought and led me to take on the challenge. My father recorded his life story when he was in his eighties; his experiences were nothing short of revelatory.

My wife Anne has shown extraordinary patience as I toiled away for many months on writing the memoir's contents, and I thank her for this. My aunt Sylvia Shire provided much information about my mother's family, and her daughter Miriam arranged several lengthy phone calls in which I was included. Their content was put on a flash drive that made for much easier recollection of life and escape from Austria. My children Elizabeth and David provided much of the stimulus to my efforts, for the book will hopefully be read not only by them but also by our grandchildren Quinn and Eve.

I have been very fortunate to work with Sarah Babb, whose editorial ability has prompted me to reflect far deeper than would otherwise have been the case. Her enthusiasm and professional skills have been enormously helpful in making me look back at my life more clearly, and have added many light touches to the rambling account that I had initially put together. Without her observations, the book would have been far more mundane.

I also wish to thank Sheila Hart, who – with similar enthusiasm and great insight – has taken responsibility for the book's design, review and production management. It has been a real pleasure to witness her creative flair and work closely with her in bringing the memoir to fruition. She and her team have produced a book that has been elegantly and speedily put together.

Finally, a word of thanks to Dr, Doug Pitts, the cardiologist who saved my life 15 years ago. He made this memoir possible!

Also by Freddie Kelvin

Clinical Imaging of the Colon and Rectum
Frederick M. Kelvin and Richard Gardiner
Raven Press 1987

Made in the USA
Columbia, SC
18 January 2023